studysync®

Reading & Writing Companion

Ancient Realms

studysync

studysync.com

Copyright © BookheadEd Learning, LLC
All Rights Reserved.

Send all inquiries to:
BookheadEd Learning, LLC
610 Daniel Young Drive
Sonoma, CA 95476

Cover, ©iStock.com/TerryJLawrence, ©iStock.com/Pakhnyushchyy, ©iStock.com/alexey_boldin, ©iStock.com/skegbydave

9 10 11 12 13 14 15 16 LWI 22 21 20 19 C

STUDENT GUIDE

GETTING STARTED

Welcome to the StudySync Reading and Writing Companion! In this booklet, you will find a collection of readings based on the theme of the unit you are studying. As you work through the readings, you will be asked to answer questions and perform a variety of tasks designed to help you closely analyze and understand each text selection. Read on for an explanation of each section of this booklet.

Student Instructions for Reading and Writing Companion

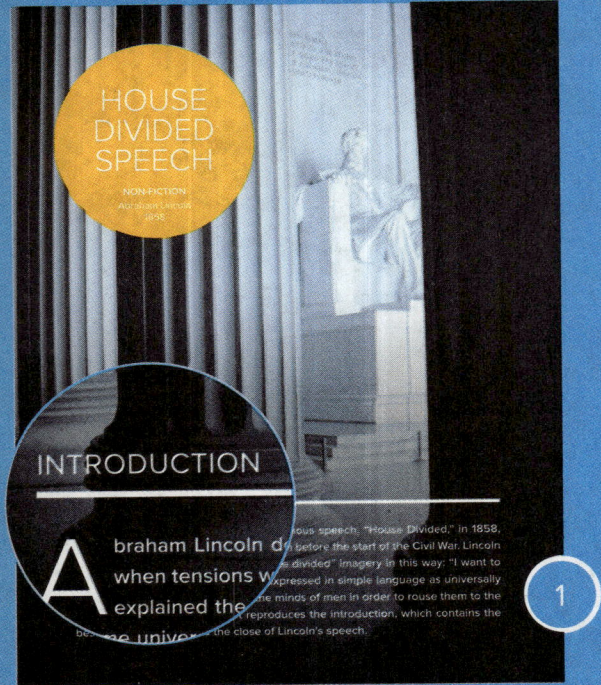

1 INTRODUCTION

An Introduction to each text provides historical context for your reading as well as information about the author. You will also learn about the genre of the excerpt and the year in which it was written.

2 FIRST READ

During your first reading of each excerpt, you should just try to get a general idea of the content and message of the reading. Don't worry if there are parts you don't understand or words that are unfamiliar to you. You'll have an opportunity later to dive deeper into the text.

Many times, while working through the Think Questions after your first read, you will be asked to **annotate** or **make annotations** about what you are reading. This means that you should use the "Notes" column to make comments or jot down any questions you may have about the text. You may also want to note any unfamiliar vocabulary words here.

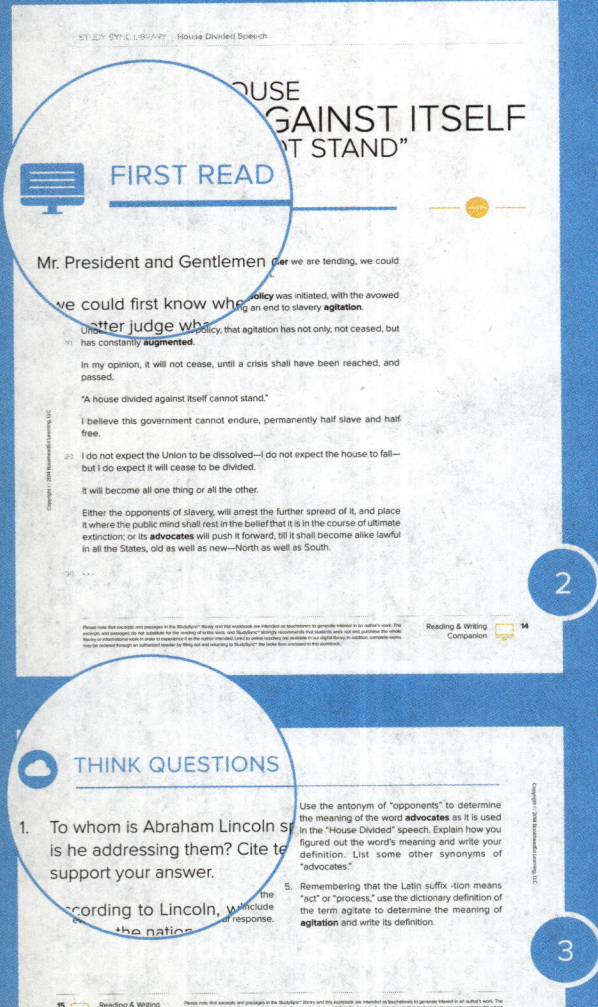

3 THINK QUESTIONS

These questions will ask you to start thinking critically about the text, asking specific questions about its purpose, and making connections to your prior knowledge and reading experiences. To answer these questions, you should go back to the text and draw upon specific evidence that you find there to support your responses. You will also begin to explore some of the more challenging vocabulary words used in the excerpt.

iv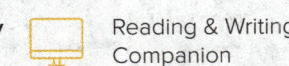

Student Instructions for Reading and Writing Companion

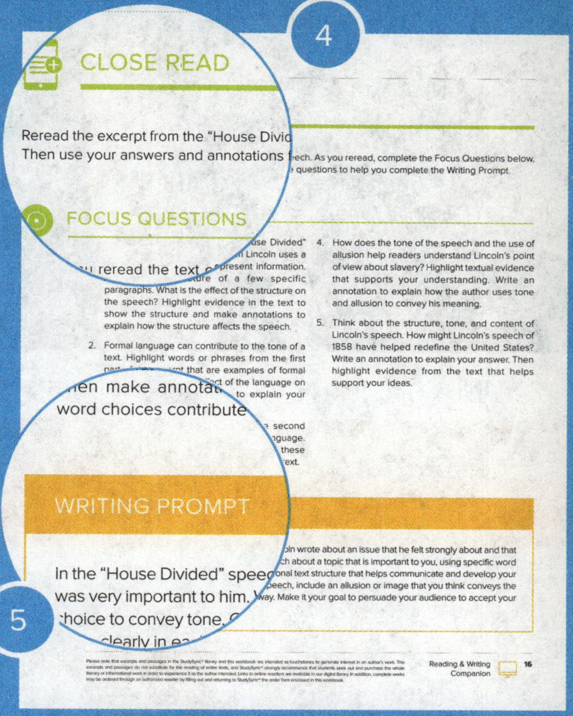

4 CLOSE READ & FOCUS QUESTIONS

After you have completed the First Read, you will then be asked to go back and read the excerpt more closely and critically. Before you begin your Close Read, you should read through the Focus Questions to get an idea of the concepts you will want to focus on during your second reading. You should work through the Focus Questions by making annotations, highlighting important concepts, and writing notes or questions in the "Notes" column. Depending on instructions from your teacher, you may need to respond online or use a separate piece of paper to start expanding on your thoughts and ideas.

5 WRITING PROMPT

Your study of each excerpt or selection will end with a writing assignment. To complete this assignment, you should use your notes, annotations, and answers to both the Think and Focus Questions. Be sure to read the prompt carefully and address each part of it in your writing assignment.

6 EXTENDED WRITING PROJECT

After you have read and worked through all of the unit text selections, you will move on to a writing project. This project will walk you through steps to plan, draft, revise, edit, and finally publish an essay or other piece of writing about one or more of the texts you have studied in the unit. Student models and graphic organizers will provide guidance and help you organize your thoughts as you plan and write your essay. Throughout the project, you will also study and work on specific writing skills to help you develop different portions of your writing.

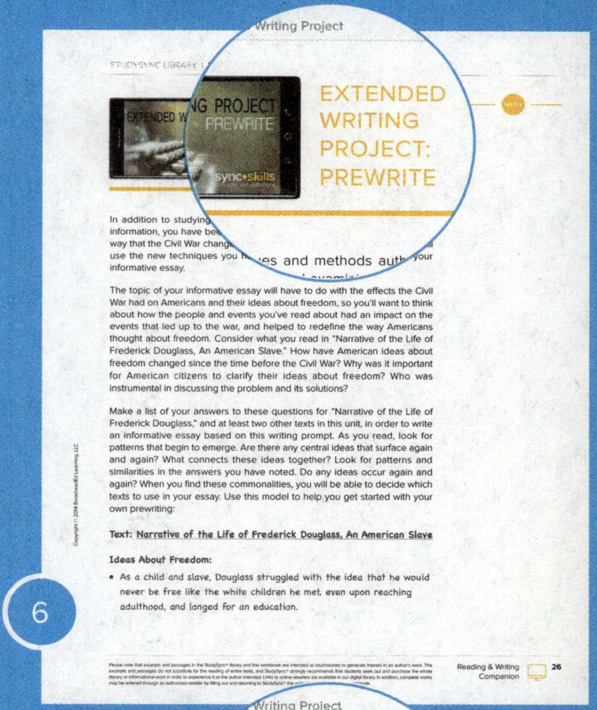

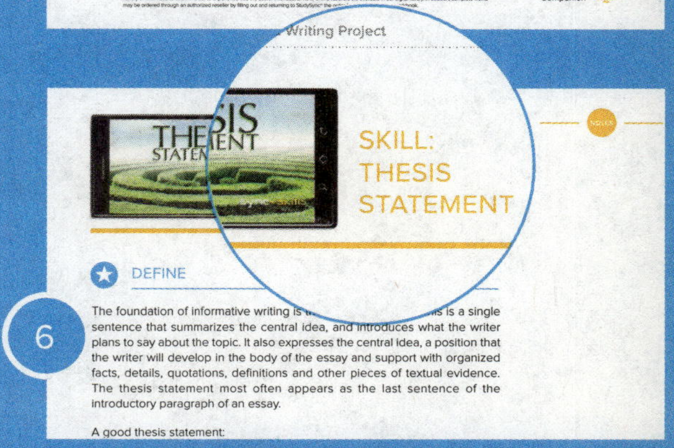

UNIT 2   How does history inform and inspire us?

Ancient Realms

 **TEXTS**

4	**Hatshepsut: His Majesty, Herself** **NON-FICTION** Catherine M. Andronik
10	**Book of the Dead** **NON-FICTION** Authors Unknown (translated by E.A. Wallis Budge)
15	**The Book of Exodus** **NON-FICTION** Authors Unknown
21	**A Short Walk Around the Pyramids & Through the World of Art** **NON-FICTION** Philip M. Isaacson
26	**Aesop's Fables** **FICTION** Aesop (translated by George Fyler Townsend)
31	**The Lightning Thief** **FICTION** Rick Riordan
37	**Perseus** **POETRY** Robert Hayden
40	**Heroes Every Child Should Know: Perseus** **FICTION** Hamilton Wright Mabie

Please note that excerpts and passages in the StudySync® library and this workbook are intended as touchstones to generate interest in an author's work. The excerpts and passages do not substitute for the reading of entire texts, and StudySync® strongly recommends that students seek out and purchase the whole literary or informational work in order to experience it as the author intended. Links to online resellers are available in our digital library. In addition, complete works may be ordered through an authorized reseller by filling out and returning to StudySync® the order form enclosed in this workbook.

TEXTS

48   Black Ships Before Troy: The Story of the Iliad
FICTION Rosemary Sutcliff

53   Mythology: Timeless Tales of Gods and Heroes
FICTION Edith Hamilton

59   The Hero Schliemann: The Dreamer Who Dug for Troy
NON-FICTION Laura Amy Schlitz

EXTENDED WRITING PROJECT

64   Extended Writing Project: Literary Analysis

68   Extended Writing Project: Prewrite

70   **SKILL:** Thesis Statement

72   **SKILL:** Organize Argumentative Writing

75   **SKILL:** Supporting Details

78   Extended Writing Project: Plan

80   **SKILL:** Introductions

82   **SKILL:** Body Paragraphs and Transitions

86   **SKILL:** Conclusions

88   Extended Writing Project: Draft

90   Extended Writing Project: Revise

92   **SKILL:** Sources and Citations

95   Extended Writing Project: Edit, Proofread, and Publish

99

Text Fulfillment through StudySync

HATSHEPSUT: HIS MAJESTY, HERSELF

NON-FICTION
Catherine M. Andronik
2001

INTRODUCTION

In Egypt's eighteenth dynasty, during the mid-to-late 1400s BCE, a long pattern of male dominance was interrupted when Hatshepsut, the widow of Pharaoh Tuthmosis II, and daughter of Tuthmosis, took the throne. Hatshepsut's reign lasted twenty-two years, during which time she built great monuments, sent an expedition to the little-known land of Punt, and handed over a peaceful Egypt to her nephew, Tuthmosis III, who subsequently attempted to erase Hatshepsut's historical imprint.

"Hatshepsut had no choice: she had to call herself pharaoh, or king—a male title."

FIRST READ

1   Hatshepsut, royal daughter of **Pharaoh** Tuthmosis and his Great Wife Ahmose, grew up in an Egypt that was peaceful, **prosperous**, and respected throughout the known world.

2   Despite this prosperity, all but one of Hatshepsut's siblings died. Fatal diseases were common, deadly creatures such as scorpions flourished in the Egyptian desert, accidents happened, and a doctor's treatment was often more superstitious than scientific. When the time came for Pharaoh Tuthmosis to name an **heir** to his throne, only one son remained: Tuthmosis, son of Mutnofret, a woman of the pharaoh's harem. When he became pharaoh, young Tuthmosis would have little choice but to marry a woman of the royal blood. Marriages between close relatives were customary within ancient Egypt's royal family, so Hatshepsut was destined to become her half brother's wife. As the sole child of the pharaoh and the God's Wife, Hatshepsut was her dynasty's last hope to keep the royal bloodlines of Egypt intact.

3   Hatshepsut's father, Pharaoh Tuthmosis I, died at the relatively old age of fifty. His secret tomb, the first underground chamber to be hidden in the towering cliffs of the Valley of the Kings, just northwest of Thebes, had been excavated years in advance. The fine sarcophagus (sar-KOFF-ah-guss), or stone coffin, which would hold his body was also ready. The pharaoh's mummy was carefully prepared, as befitted a great and beloved king. After seventy days, with solemn ceremony, Tuthmosis was laid in a tomb filled with all the choice food and drink, games and furniture, clothing and jewelry, and the little clay servant figures, called shawabtis (shah-WAHB-tees), that he could possibly need in the afterlife.

4   Following her father's death, Hatshepsut married her half brother, and the young man was crowned Pharaoh Tuthmosis II. Hatshepsut may have been only about twelve years old. As queen, she received a variety of new titles. Her favorite was God's Wife. Tuthmosis II and Hatshepsut had one child, a daughter named Neferure (neh-feh-ROO-ray).

5. The reign of Tuthmosis II was unremarkable. It was also brief, for he was a sickly young man. Within a few years of his coronation, Hatshepsut's husband had died.

6. With the death of Tuthmosis II, Egypt was left without a king to ensure that the many gods would look kindly upon the fragile desert land. Maat was a delicate thing, and without a pharaoh to tend to its preservation, it was in danger of collapsing.

7. Although Hatshepsut had been Tuthmosis II's Great Wife, he'd had other wives in his harem, including one named Isis. Isis had borne the pharaoh a baby boy, who was also named Tuthmosis. Since Isis was not royal, neither was her baby. But like his father, he could grow up to be pharaoh if he married a princess of the royal blood: his half sister, Neferure.

8. Until Tuthmosis III was mature enough to be crowned pharaoh what Egypt needed was a regent, an adult who could take control of the country. The regent would have to be someone familiar with palace life and protocol. He would need to conduct himself with the proper authority around the royal advisors. He should be prepared to wield power if it became necessary, and he should feel comfortable around visiting dignitaries from other lands. He needed to know his place among the priests of the various gods.

9. It was a job Hatshepsut, perhaps just fifteen years old, had been training for since her earliest days by her father's side. Women had acted as regents for infants at other times in Egypt's history, and the gods had not frowned upon them.

10. So until Tuthmosis III was ready to be crowned as pharaoh, the acting ruler of Egypt would be his aunt, the royal widow of the king, Hatshepsut.

11. At first, little Tuthmosis III was considered the pharaoh, with Hatshepsut just his second-in-command. But a small child could not be an effective ruler. As Hatshepsut settled into her role as regent, she gradually took on more and more of the royal decision-making. She appointed officials and advisors; dealt with the priests; appeared in public ceremonies first behind, then beside, and eventually in front of her nephew. Gradually, over seven years, her power and influence grew. In the end, Hatshepsut was ruling Egypt in all but name.

12. There is no reliable record of exactly when or how it happened, but at some point, Hatshepsut took a bold and unprecedented step: She had herself crowned pharaoh with the large, heavy, red-and-white double crown of the two Egypts, north and south. Since all pharaohs took a throne name, a sort of symbolic name, upon their coronation, Hatshepsut chose Maatkare (maht-KAH-ray). Maat, that crucial cosmic order, was important to Hatshepsut. Egypt

required a strong pharaoh to ensure maat. Hatshepsut could be that pharaoh—even if she did happen to be a woman.

13. A few women had tried to rule Egypt before, but never with such a valid hclaim to the throne or at such a time of peace and prosperity. When Queens Nitocris and Sobekneferu had come to the throne in earlier dynasties, Egypt had been suffering from political problems, and there had been no male heirs. These women had not ruled long or well, and neither had had the audacity to proclaim herself pharaoh. Hatshepsut would be different.

14. There was no word in the language of ancient Egypt for a female ruler; a queen was simply the wife of a king. Hatshepsut had no choice: she had to call herself pharaoh, or king—a male title. She was concerned with preserving and continuing traditional order as much as possible, so to the people of Egypt she made herself look like a man in her role as pharaoh. In ceremonies, she wore a man's short kilt instead of a woman's long dress, much as she had as a child. Around her neck she wore a king's broad collar. She even fastened a false golden beard to her chin. When she wrote about herself as pharaoh, sometimes she referred to herself as he, other times as she. This would be very confusing for historians trying to uncover her identity thousands of years later.

15. Since Hatshepsut could not marry a queen, her daughter Neferure acted as God's Wife in public rituals. It was good training for Neferure, who would in time be expected to marry her half brother, Tuthmosis III, and be his royal consort. But Hatshepsut never seems to have considered that her daughter could succeed her as pharaoh.

16. Hatshepsut might have had to look and act like a man in public, but she never gave up feminine pleasures. Archaeologists have uncovered bracelets and alabaster cosmetic pots with Hatshepsut's cartouche (kar-TOOSH), or hieroglyphic name symbol, inscribed on each. Both men and women in Egypt used **cosmetics**.They needed creams and oils to keep their skin and hair from drying out under the brutal desert sun. And the kohl, a kind of makeup made from powdered lead that people applied around their eyes, did more than make them attractive; it also helped block out the sun's glare. But Hatshepsut was especially particular about her appearance. One inscription describes her as "more beautiful than anything."

17. With the exception of one military campaign against Nubia, Hatshepsut's reign was peaceful. Instead of expanding Egypt's borders through war and conquest, Hatshepsut built **monuments** within her country to proclaim its power. Her masterpiece was the magnificent temple at the site known today as Deir el-Bahri. The temple was dedicated to Amen, the god who was supposed to be the divine father of every pharaoh, the god to whom

STUDYSYNC LIBRARY | Hatshepsut: His Majesty, Herself

Hatshepsut felt she owed her good fortune. The temple at Deir el-Bahri was said to be Hatshepsut's own mortuary temple. The building is set into the side of a mountain and rises gracefully in three beautifully proportioned tiers, each supported by columns like those to be seen centuries later in Greek temples. Its design was far ahead of its time. Hatshepsut called it Djeser-Djeseru (JEH-sir jeh-SEH-roo)—"Holy of Holies."

13. On the walls of this temple, Hatshepsut had artists carve and paint her biography. According to the story told on the walls of Djeser-Djeseru, she had been chosen as pharaoh by the gods themselves, even before her birth. Perhaps, even after years on the throne, she still felt a need to justify a woman's right to rule. The gods in the pictures on the temple walls do not seem to care whether Hatshepsut is a man or a woman—in fact, some of the paintings show her as a boy.

© 2001 by Catherine M. Andronik, reproduced by permission of Catherine M. Andronik.

THINK QUESTIONS

1. Before Hatshepsut became pharaoh, what practice does the text say she had for the job? Include evidence from the text to support your answer.

2. How was Hatshepsut's reign different from the reigns of the two earlier queens who had ruled Egypt? Use evidence from the text to support your answer.

3. What evidence does the text give to support the idea that Hatshepsut cared about her appearance?

4. Use context to determine the meaning of the word **cosmetics** as it is used in *Hatshepsut, His Majesty, Herself*. Write your definition of "cosmetics" and tell how you got it. How are the words "creams," "oils," and "kohl" in the following sentences related to the vocabulary word? How does this relationship help you better understand the meaning of "cosmetics"?

5. Remembering that the Latin suffix *-ous* means "having, characterized by," use the context clues provided in the passage to determine the meaning of **prosperous**. Write your definition of "prosperous" and tell how you got it. In your answer, identify any words you know that seem to be related to "prosperous," and explain how these relationships helped you infer the word's meaning.

STUDYSYNC LIBRARY | Hatshepsut: His Majesty, Herself

CLOSE READ

Reread the excerpt from *Hatshepsut: His Majesty, Herself*. As you reread, complete the Focus Questions below. Then use your answers and annotations from the questions to help you complete the Writing Prompt.

FOCUS QUESTIONS

1. The focus of *Hatshepsut: His Majesty, Herself* is on an individual, Hatshepsut. The first two paragraphs introduce her. What information does the second paragraph give about the special destiny that awaited Hatshepsut? Why was that her destiny? Highlight textual evidence and make annotations to explain your ideas.

2. Paragraphs 8–11 talk about what a regent in ancient Egypt was expected to be like, and they describe Hatshepsut's behavior as regent. What details show that Hatshepsut successfully did what a regent was expected to do? Highlight evidence from the text and make annotations to support your explanation.

3. What does the way Hatshepsut became pharaoh show about her character? Highlight details from the text and make annotations to show how they provide evidence for your answer.

4. Paragraph 14 provides many details about ways in which Hatshepsut made herself look like a man in public. Highlight two or more of those details. Why did she choose to appear like a man in public? Highlight textual evidence and make annotations to explain your answer.

5. Paragraphs 17–18 provide examples of the ways in which Hatshepsut used her reign to declare Egypt's power. What do the choices Hatshepsut made say about her a ruler? Highlight textual evidence and make annotations to explain your answer.

WRITING PROMPT

How is a historical figure like Hatshepsut relevant today? In what ways can she be considered an inspiration for both boys and girls? What specific events or situations in Hatshepsut's life does the author use to introduce, illustrate, and elaborate on her character and values? Write a clear and well-organized explanation that examines why Hatshepsut continues to be relevant. Develop the topic and support your ideas with facts, details, quotations, or other evidence from the text.

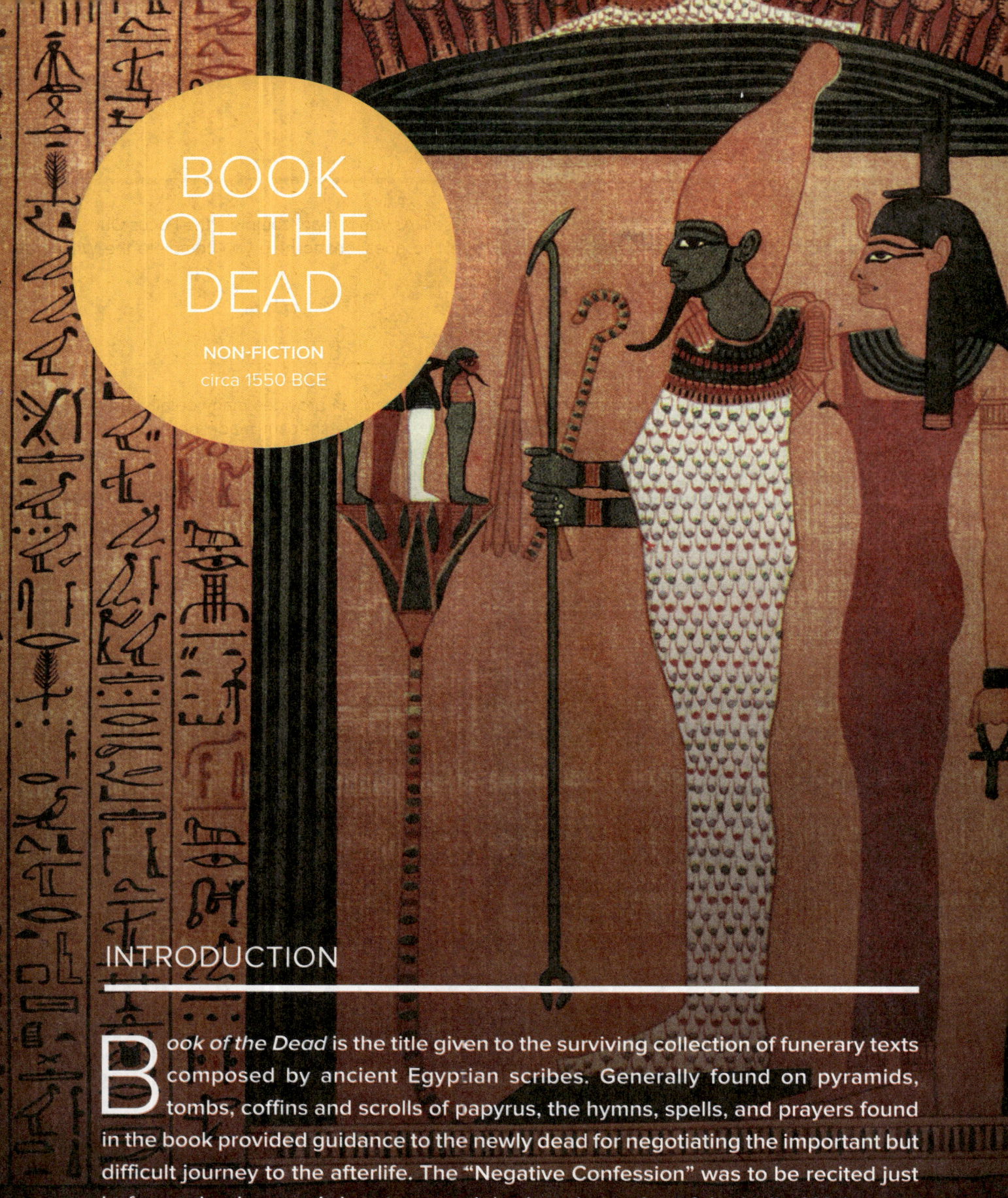

BOOK OF THE DEAD

NON-FICTION
circa 1550 BCE

INTRODUCTION

Book of the Dead is the title given to the surviving collection of funerary texts composed by ancient Egyptian scribes. Generally found on pyramids, tombs, coffins and scrolls of papyrus, the hymns, spells, and prayers found in the book provided guidance to the newly dead for negotiating the important but difficult journey to the afterlife. The "Negative Confession" was to be recited just before a dead person's heart was weighed on the scales of the Hall of Ma'at

"I have wronged none, I have done no evil."

FIRST READ

The Negative Confession
From the Papyrus of Ani:

1. Hail, Usekh-nemmt, who comest forth from Anu, I have not committed sin.
2. Hail, Hept-khet, who comest forth from Kher-aha, I have not committed robbery with violence.
3. Hail, Fenti, who comest forth from Khemenu, I have not stolen.
4. Hail, Am-khaibit, who comest forth from Qernet, I have not slain men and women.
5. Hail, Neha-her, who comest forth from Rasta, I have not stolen grain.
6. Hail, Ruruti, who comest forth from heaven, I have not **purloined** offerings.
7. Hail, Arfi-em-khet, who comest forth from Suat, I have not stolen the property of God.
8. Hail, Neba, who comest and goest, I have not uttered lies.
9. Hail, Set-qesu, who comest forth from Hensu, I have not carried away food.
10. Hail, Utu-nesert, who comest forth from Het-ka-Ptah, I have not uttered curses.
11. Hail, Qerrti, who comest forth from Amentet, I have not committed adultery, I have not lain with men.
12. Hail, Her-f-ha-f, who comest forth from thy cavern, I have made none to weep.
13. Hail, Basti, who comest forth from Bast, I have not eaten the heart.
14. Hail, Ta-retiu, who comest forth from the night, I have not attacked any man.
15. Hail, Unem-snef, who comest forth from the execution chamber, I am not a man of **deceit**.
16. Hail, Unem-besek, who comest forth from Mabit, I have not stolen **cultivated** land.

17. Hail, Neb-Maat, who comest forth from Maati, I have not been an eavesdropper.
18. Hail, Tenemiu, who comest forth from Bast, I have not **slandered** [no man].
19. Hail, Sertiu, who comest forth from Anu, I have not been angry without just cause.
20. Hail, Tutu, who comest forth from Ati (the Busirite Nome), I have not debauched the wife of any man.
21. Hail, Uamenti, who comest forth from the Khebt chamber, I have not debauched the wife of [any] man.
22. Hail, Maa-antuf, who comest forth from Per-Menu, I have not polluted myself.
23. Hail, Her-uru, who comest forth from Nehatu, I have terrorized none.
24. Hail, Khemiu, who comest forth from Kaui, I have not **transgressed** [the law].
25. Hail, Shet-kheru, who comest forth from Urit, I have not been wroth.
26. Hail, Nekhenu, who comest forth from Heqat, I have not shut my ears to the words of truth.
27. Hail, Kenemti, who comest forth from Kenmet, I have not **blasphemed**.
28. Hail, An-hetep-f, who comest forth from Sau, I am not a man of violence.
29. Hail, Sera-kheru, who comest forth from Unaset, I have not been a stirrer up of strife.
30. Hail, Neb-heru, who comest forth from Netchfet, I have not acted with undue haste.
31. Hail, Sekhriu, who comest forth from Uten, I have not pried into matters.
32. Hail, Neb-abui, who comest forth from Sauti, I have not multiplied my words in speaking.
33. Hail, Nefer-Tem, who comest forth from Het-ka-Ptah, I have wronged none, I have done no evil.
34. Hail, Tem-Sepu, who comest forth from Tetu, I have not worked witchcraft against the king.
35. Hail, Ari-em-ab-f, who comest forth from Tebu, I have never stopped [the flow of] water.
36. Hail, Ahi, who comest forth from Nu, I have never raised my voice.
37. Hail, Uatch-rekhit, who comest forth from Sau, I have not cursed God.
38. Hail, Neheb-ka, who comest forth from thy cavern, I have not acted with **arrogance**.

39. Hail, Neheb-nefert, who comest forth from thy cavern, I have not stolen the bread of the gods.
40. Hail, Tcheser-tep, who comest forth from the shrine, I have not carried away the khenfu cakes from the Spirits of the dead.
41. Hail, An-af, who comest forth from Maati, I have not snatched away the bread of the child, nor treated with **contempt** the god of my city.
42. Hail, Hetch-abhu, who comest forth from Ta-she (the Fayyum), I have not slain the cattle belonging to the god.

 THINK QUESTIONS

1. Using textual evidence, explain why this text is called "The Negative Confession."

2. Cite details from the text to explain how these confessions convey the values of the Egyptians.

3. Using textual evidence, support the idea that the speaker seeks to avoid punishment in the afterlife.

4. Use context clues to determine the meaning of the word **purloined** as it is used in confession Number 6 in *Book of the Dead*. Write your definition of "purloined," and tell how you arrived at it.

5. Noting that many of the confessions address the speaker's words as well as his actions, use the context clues provided in the passage to infer the meaning of **blasphemed**. Write your definition of "blasphemed," and tell how you arrived at it. Check your definition against an online or print dictionary and revise as needed.

STUDYSYNC LIBRARY | **Book of the Dead**

CLOSE READ

Reread the excerpt from *Book of the Dead*. As you reread, complete the Focus Questions below. Then use your answers and annotations from the questions to help you complete the Writing Prompt.

FOCUS QUESTIONS

1. What do confessions 15, 17, and 26 have in common? What do they tell you about the laws of the Egyptian gods? Highlight textual evidence and write annotations to explain your response.

2. What idea about theft can be inferred from the confessions? What do the statements about theft suggest about the text's central idea? Highlight specific confessions from the text that provide evidence and write annotations to explain your response.

3. What idea about anger and the inability to control one's emotions can be inferred from the confessions? What do the statements about anger suggest about the text's central idea? Cite textual evidence and write annotations to explain your response.

4. The sin of arrogance is well documented in ancient texts. Which confessions are related to arrogance or pride against the gods? Highlight textual evidence and write annotations that explain your choices.

5. How do confessions 27, 37, 39, and 42 support the ideas stated in confession 41? How do they help inform the reader's understanding of the laws of the Egyptian gods? Cite specific evidence from the text, and write annotations to explain your response.

WRITING PROMPT

Reread confessions 12 to 42 of "The Negative Confession." Analyze the details, choosing eight confessions, with details that together suggest a similar central idea. Summarize the central idea in your own words, and use textual evidence that supports your thinking.

THE BOOK OF EXODUS

NON-FICTION
circa 1400 BCE

INTRODUCTION

The second book of the Pentateuch, the Book of Exodus chronicles the Israelites' escape from slavery in Egypt and their difficult passage through the wilderness to the land of Canaan. After leading his people to safety, Moses climbed Mt. Sinai, where God spoke to him from the heavens and established a covenant. The two stone tablets that Moses brought down, inscribed with the Ten Commandments, went on to become the basis for Judaic law.

STUDYSYNC LIBRARY | The Book of Exodus

"…Moses spoke, and God answered him in thunder."

FIRST READ

Chapter 18

1 Jethro, the priest of Mid'ian, Moses' father-in-law, heard of all that God had done for Moses and for Israel his people, how the LORD had brought Israel out of Egypt. **2** Now Jethro, Moses' father-in-law, had taken Zippo'rah, Moses' wife, after he had sent her away, **3** and her two sons, of whom the name of the one was Gershom (for he said, "I have been a sojourner in a foreign land"), **4** and the name of the other, Elie'zer (for he said, "The God of my father was my help, and delivered me from the sword of Pharaoh"). **5** And Jethro, Moses' father-in-law, came with his sons and his wife to Moses in the wilderness where he was encamped at the mountain of God. **6** And when one told Moses, "Lo, your father-in-law Jethro is coming to you with your wife and her two sons with her," **7** Moses went out to meet his father-in-law, and did obeisance and kissed him; and they asked each other of their welfare, and went into the tent. **8** Then Moses told his father-in-law all that the LORD had done to Pharaoh and to the Egyptians for Israel's sake, all the hardship that had come upon them in the way, and how the LORD had delivered them. **9** And Jethro rejoiced for all the good which the LORD had done to Israel, in that he had delivered them out of the hand of the Egyptians.

10 And Jethro said, "Blessed be the LORD, who has delivered you out of the hand of the Egyptians and out of the hand of Pharaoh. **11** Now I know that the LORD is greater than all gods, because he delivered the people from under the hand of the Egyptians, when they dealt arrogantly with them." **12** And Jethro, Moses' father-in-law, offered a burnt offering and sacrifices to God; and Aaron came with all the elders of Israel to eat bread with Moses' father-in-law before God.

13 On the morrow Moses sat to judge the people, and the people stood about Moses from morning till evening. **14** When Moses' father-in-law saw all that he was doing for the people, he said, "What is this that you are doing for the people? Why do you sit alone, and all the people stand about you from morning till evening?" **15** And Moses said to his father-in-law, "Because the

people come to me to **inquire** of God; **16** when they have a dispute, they come to me and I decide between a man and his neighbor, and I make them know the **statutes** of God and his decisions." **17** Moses' father-in-law said to him, "What you are doing is not good. **18** You and the people with you will wear yourselves out, for the thing is too heavy for you; you are not able to perform it alone. **19** Listen now to my voice; I will give you counsel, and God be with you! You shall represent the people before God; and bring their cases to God; **20** and you shall teach them the statutes and the decisions, and make them know the way in which they must walk and what they must do. **21** Moreover choose able men from all the people, such as fear God, men who are trustworthy and who hate a bribe; and place such men over the people as rulers of thousands, of hundreds, of fifties, and of tens. **22** And let them judge the people at all times; every great matter they shall bring to you, but any small matter they shall decide themselves; so it will be easier for you, and they will bear the **burden** with you. **23** If you do this, and God so commands you, then you will be able to endure, and all these people also will go to their place in peace."
24 So Moses gave heed to the voice of his father-in-law and did all that he had said. **25** Moses chose able men out of all Israel, and made them heads over the people, rulers of thousands, of hundreds, of fifties, and of tens. **26** And they judged the people at all times; hard cases they brought to Moses, but any small matter they decided themselves. 27 Then Moses let his father-in-law depart, and he went his way to his own country.

Chapter 19

1 On the third new moon after the people of Israel had gone forth out of the land of Egypt, on that day they came into the wilderness of Sinai. **2** And when they set out from Reph'idim and came into the wilderness of Sinai, they **encamped** in the wilderness; and there Israel encamped before the mountain. **3** And Moses went up to God, and the LORD called to him out of the mountain, saying, "Thus you shall say to the house of Jacob, and tell the people of Israel: **4** You have seen what I did to the Egyptians, and how I bore you on eagles' wings and brought you to myself. **5** Now therefore, if you will obey my voice and keep my **covenant,** you shall be my own possession among all peoples; for all the earth is mine, **6** and you shall be to me a kingdom of priests and a holy nation. These are the words which you shall speak to the children of Israel."
7 So Moses came and called the elders of the people, and set before them all these words which the LORD had commanded him. **8** And all the people answered together and said, "All that the LORD has spoken we will do." And Moses reported the words of the people to the LORD. **9** And the LORD said to Moses, "Lo, I am coming to you in a thick cloud, that the people may hear when I speak with you, and may also believe you for ever."

16 On the morning of the third day there were thunders and lightnings, and a thick cloud upon the mountain, and a very loud trumpet blast, so that all the people who were in the camp trembled. **17** Then Moses brought the people out of the camp to meet God; and they took their stand at the foot of the mountain. **18** And Mount Sinai was wrapped in smoke, because the LORD descended upon it in fire; and the smoke of it went up like the smoke of a kiln, and the whole mountain quaked greatly. **19** And as the sound of the trumpet grew louder and louder, Moses spoke, and God answered him in thunder. **20** And the LORD came down upon Mount Sinai, to the top of the mountain; and the LORD called Moses to the top of the mountain, and Moses went up.

Chapter 20

1 And God spoke all these words, saying,
2 "I am the LORD your God, who brought you out of the land of Egypt, out of the house of bondage.
3 "You shall have no other gods before me.
4 "You shall not make for yourself a graven image, or any likeness of anything that is in heaven above, or that is in the earth beneath, or that is in the water under the earth; **5** you shall not bow down to them or serve them; for I the LORD your God am a jealous God, visiting the iniquity of the fathers upon the children to the third and the fourth generation of those who hate me, **6** but showing steadfast love to thousands of those who love me and keep my commandments.
7 "You shall not take the name of the LORD your God in vain; for the LORD will not hold him guiltless who takes his name in vain.
8 "Remember the Sabbath day, to keep it holy. **9** Six days you shall labor, and do all your work; **10** but the seventh day is a Sabbath to the LORD your God; in it you shall not do any work, you, or your son, or your daughter, your manservant, or your maidservant, or your cattle, or the sojourner who is within your gates; **11** for in six days the LORD made heaven and earth, the sea, and all that is in them, and rested the seventh day; therefore the LORD blessed the Sabbath day and hallowed it.
12 "Honor your father and your mother, that your days may be long in the land which the LORD your God gives you.
13 "You shall not kill.
14 "You shall not commit adultery.
15 "You shall not steal.
16 "You shall not bear false witness against your neighbor.
17 "You shall not covet your neighbor's house; you shall not covet your neighbor's wife, or his manservant, or his maidservant, or his ox, or his ass, or anything that is your neighbor's."
18 Now when all the people perceived the thunderings and the lightnings and the sound of the trumpet and the mountain smoking, the people were afraid and trembled; and they stood afar off, **19** and said to Moses, "You speak

to us, and we will hear; but let not God speak to us, lest we die." **20** And Moses said to the people, "Do not fear; for God has come to prove you, and that the fear of him may be before your eyes, that you may not sin."
21 And the people stood afar off, while Moses drew near to the thick darkness where God was. **22** And the LORD said to Moses, "Thus you shall say to the people of Israel: 'You have seen for yourselves that I have talked with you from heaven.

THINK QUESTIONS

1. What crucial advice does Jethro provide, and how does it affect Moses and the Israelites? Cite relevant textual evidence in your answer.

2. The Lord declares that he wants to make the Israelites his "possession among all peoples." What does the Lord mean? What will the Israelites need to do in order to become the Lord's "possession"? Cite textual evidence to support your explanation.

3. How do the people respond when God comes to them on the mountain? Why do they respond that way? Cite textual evidence in your answer.

4. Use context clues to determine the meaning of the word **inquire** as it is used in the Book of Exodus. Write your definition of "inquire," and tell how you arrived at it.

5. Remembering that the Latin prefix *en-* means "to cause to be," use the context clues provided in the passage to determine the meaning of **encamped.** Write your definition of "encamped," and tell how you arrived at it.

STUDYSYNC LIBRARY | **The Book of Exodus**

CLOSE READ

Reread the excerpt from the Book of Exodus. As you reread, complete the Focus Questions below. Then use your answers and annotations from the questions to help you complete the Writing Prompt.

FOCUS QUESTIONS

1. Highlight details from the text in Chapter 18, verses 1–6, that introduce and illustrate Jethro's visit. What details explain Jethro's role in Moses' life? Make annotations and cite evidence from the text to explain your response.

2. How do the events described in verses 3–6 of Chapter 19 help readers understand that Moses has a special role to play in the history of the Israelites? Highlight textual evidence and annotate your ideas.

3. Highlight details in Chapter 19, verses 16–20, that describe the physical surroundings of Moses and the Israelites. What impact do the details have on these individuals? How do they help the reader interpret the events being described? Highlight textual evidence and annotate your ideas.

4. Reread Chapter 20, verses 8–11. Highlight and annotate the verse that states a central idea and the verses that provide supporting details. Then jot down reasons to explain your choices. Cite evidence from the text to explain your response.

5. Discuss the historical significance of the Ten Commandments that God delivers to Moses. How do they serve to inform the people of Israel? Throughout the ages, how have they continued to inform others? Highlight textual evidence and annotate your ideas.

WRITING PROMPT

Use your understanding of informational text elements to determine how individuals, ideas, and events interact in the Book of Exodus. Choose an important individual, event, or idea from the text and demonstrate how one influences the other elements. How does this interaction ultimately lead to the delivery of the Ten Commandments? Cite specific textual evidence to support your ideas.

A SHORT WALK AROUND THE PYRAMIDS
& THROUGH THE WORLD OF ART

NON-FICTION
Philip M. Isaacson
1993

INTRODUCTION

Philip Isaacson's book shows the rewards of looking closely at art. He explains how color and style affect the way images are perceived, and reinforces his assertions with illustrations. Here he shows readers how to look at the pyramids and several sculptures in the way an artist would.

"When you walk among them, you walk in a place made for giants."

FIRST READ

A SIMPLE FORM

1. At Giza, a few miles north of Saqqara, sit three great pyramids, each named for the king—or Pharaoh—during whose reign it was built. No other buildings are so well known, yet the first sight of them sitting in their field is breathtaking. When you walk among them, you walk in a place made for giants. They seem too large to have been made by human beings, too perfect to have been formed by nature, and when the sun is overhead, not solid enough to be attached to the sand. In the minutes before sunrise, they are the color of faded roses, and when the last rays of the desert sun touch them, they turn to amber. But whatever the light, their broad **proportions**, the beauty of the limestone, and the care with which it is fitted into place create three unforgettable works of art.

2. What do we learn about art when we look at the pyramids?

3. First, when all of the things that go into a work—its **components**—complement one another, they create an object that has a certain spirit, and we can call that spirit harmony. The pyramids are **harmonious** because limestone, a warm, quiet material, is a cordial companion for a simple, logical, pleasing shape. In fact, the stone and the shape are so comfortable with each other that the pyramids seem inevitable—as though they were bound to have the form, color, and texture that they do have.

4. The pyramids also show us that simple things must be made with care. The fine workmanship that went into the building of the pyramids is a part of their beauty. Complicated shapes may conceal poor work—such shapes distract our eye—but in something as simple as a pyramid, there is no way to hide flaws. Because any flaw would mar its beauty, the craftsmanship must be perfect.... Any building less beautifully designed or made with less skill would have looked awkward in the company of the dignified old structures near it.

5. Finally, pyramids show us that a light helps to shape our feelings about art. As the sun moves above the desert, the pyramids seem to change. As they do, our feelings about them also change. In the early morning they sit squarely on the horizon, and we feel that they have become the kings for which they were named; by midday they have become restless and change into silver-white clouds; and at dusk they settle down and regain their power.

6. The pyramids will always work their magic on us. Their forms, so simple and reasonable, and their great size lift us high above the ordinary moments in our lives.

SCULPTURE

7. As we have seen, art does not have to be complicated to be wonderful. Still, art can be more complicated, often much more complicated, than the pyramids at Saqqara and Giza.

8. We are looking at a piece of sculpture—the head of a horse carved in marble the color of cream. But it's more than a horse. It represents the Greek goddess of the moon, Selene, as she drops from the night into a dark sea. The horse was carved about 435 B.C. for a temple on a hill in the ancient city of Athens.

9. The temple is called the Parthenon, and the horse was part of a group of figures made especially for its east pediment, a large stone triangle fitted just under the roof. The Parthenon, high on a hill, catches the first light of morning. The carvers wanted the sight of that golden light washing across the horse and a line of other gods to be unforgettable. And so they coaxed the images of their gods out of the marble with such tenderness that they gave the world an example of ideal beauty....

10. The traditional art of African nations is a wonderful part of the world's art. Like the art of all people who live in groups called tribes—the people of the Pacific islands, the Native Americans, the Eskimos, the Indians of the Northwest Coast of Canada—it was once called **primitive** art. But it isn't primitive. It isn't primitive in its shape or in the way it is made or in the deep feelings it expresses. There doesn't seem to be a good short name for the traditional art of tribal societies, but that's not important. We should enjoy it, as we enjoy all art, because of its form, its color, its materials, and its beautiful workmanship, and for what we may know of the people who made it....

11. Most of the things that we have considered so far have three dimensions: height, width, and thickness. They have been buildings and sculpture, solid things that we can reach out and touch. Some are very simple forms. Others are more complicated. Sculpture that doesn't look real we called **abstract** and said it sometimes stood for things that we can see and sometimes for things we can only sense. All that we have seen has given us a sense of

harmony and has touched our emotions. We found harmony when design, materials, and craftsmanship joined to become an agreeable whole. And we learned that harmony alone does not make a wonderful work of art. Art must also stir our emotions, and it can do this in many ways. The three great pyramids did this through their colossal size and their dramatic seat on the edge of the desert. The Elgin Marbles and the Kota figure achieved it by carrying the deep spiritual feelings of their artists to us.

Excerpted from *A Short Walk Around the Pyramids & Through the World of Art* by Philip M. Isaacson, published by Alfred A. Knopf.

THINK QUESTIONS

1. What is the author's opinion regarding the pyramids at Giza? Use textual evidence to support your answer.

2. According to the author, what three things do spectators learn about art when looking at the pyramids? Support your answer with evidence from the text.

3. Why does the author think that "primitive" is not a good description for the traditional art of tribal societies? Cite textual evidence to support your answer.

4. Use context to determine the meaning of the word **components** as it is used in *A Walk Around the Pyramids & Through the World of Art*. Write your definition of "components," and tell how you arrived at it. Then, use a dictionary to check your meaning and revise it, if necessary.

5. Use context clues to determine the meaning of the word **abstract** as it is used in *A Walk Around the Pyramids & Through the World of Art*. Write your definition of "abstract," and tell how you arrived at it.

STUDYSYNC LIBRARY | A Short Walk Around the Pyramids & Through the World of Art

 CLOSE READ

Reread the excerpt from *A Walk Among the Pyramids*. As you reread, complete the Focus Questions below. Then use your answers and annotations from the questions to help you complete the Writing Prompt.

 FOCUS QUESTIONS

1. In paragraph 3, Isaacson writes that limestone is a "cordial companion" for the simple, logical shape of the pyramids. This technique—in which the author describes an object as having human qualities—is called personification. If necessary, consult an online or print dictionary to determine the definition of "cordial." Then annotate ideas that help you explain Isaacson's meaning within the context of his argument. Identify and highlight specific evidence from the text that supports your response.

2. In paragraph 4, Isaacson uses the contrasting words "complicated" and "simple" to make a point about craftsmanship. Highlight evidence from the text that helps you explain how the relationship between these words supports Isaacson's argument, and make annotations noting your ideas.

3. In paragraph 6, Isaacson concludes his argument about the pyramids by stating that the great size of the pyramids lifts viewers "high above the ordinary moments" of their lives. How does this concluding statement both support and extend Isaacson's argument? Identify and highlight specific evidence from the text that supports your ideas.

4. In paragraph 9, what claim does Isaacson make about Greek sculpture? Highlight specific evidence from the text that he offers, and use the annotation tool to note the supporting reason for his claim that he implies.

5. How can examples of "unforgettable works of art" like the pyramids, both inform and inspire us? Cite specific evidence from the text that supports your ideas.

WRITING PROMPT

Isaacson makes the argument that the pyramids at Giza serve as timeless instructors to the masses about the elements of great art. Do you find Isaacson's argument about the qualities and impact of the pyramids persuasive? Why or why not? Explain Isaacson's argument, including the relationship between his claim, reasons, and evidence. Use your understanding of argument and claim to evaluate Isaacson's text. Support your writing with evidence from the text.

AESOP'S FABLES

FICTION
Aesop
circa 600 BCE

INTRODUCTION

There are facts and fictions surrounding the person known as Aesop. Said to be an African slave freed for his wit and intelligence, and reportedly thrown to his death over a precipice by the people of Delphi, Aesop is credited with creating hundreds of fables, though none of his actual writings survive. What can't be disputed is that the short, charming tales of wisdom and folly have left an indelible mark on Western culture. In this selection of seven fables, not all have explicit morals; some you have to figure out.

"The Ants inquired of him, 'Why did you not treasure up food during the summer?'"

FIRST READ

The Swollen Fox

1   A VERY HUNGRY FOX, seeing some bread and meat left by shepherds in the hollow of an oak, crept into the hole and made a hearty meal. When he finished, he was so full that he was not able to get out, and began to groan and lament his fate. Another Fox passing by heard his cries, and coming up, inquired the cause of his complaining. On learning what had happened, he said to him, "Ah, you will have to remain there, my friend, until you become such as you were when you crept in, and then you will easily get out."

The Flies And The Honey-Pot

2   A NUMBER of Flies were attracted to a jar of honey which had been overturned in a housekeeper's room, and placing their feet in it, ate greedily. Their feet, however, became so smeared with the honey that they could not use their wings, nor release themselves, and were suffocated. Just as they were expiring, they exclaimed, "O foolish creatures that we are, for the sake of a little pleasure we have destroyed ourselves." Pleasure bought with pains, hurts.

The Hen And The Golden Eggs

3   A COTTAGER and his wife had a Hen that laid a golden egg every day. They supposed that the Hen must contain a great lump of gold in its inside, and in order to get the gold they killed it. Having done so, they found to their surprise that the Hen differed in no respect from their other hens. The foolish pair, thus hoping to become rich all at once, **deprived** themselves of the gain of which they were assured day by day.

The Miser

4   A MISER sold all that he had and bought a lump of gold, which he buried in a hole in the ground by the side of an old wall and went to look at daily. One of his workmen observed his frequent visits to the spot and decided to watch his movements. He soon discovered the secret of the hidden treasure, and

digging down, came to the lump of gold, and stole it. The Miser, on his next visit, found the hole empty and began to tear his hair and to make loud lamentations. A neighbor, seeing him overcome with grief and learning the cause, said, "Pray do not grieve so; but go and take a stone, and place it in the hole, and fancy that the gold is still lying there. It will do you quite the same service; for when the gold was there, you had it not, as you did not make the slightest use of it."

The Fox And The Woodcutter

5   A FOX, running before the hounds, came across a Woodcutter felling an oak and begged him to show him a safe hiding-place. The Woodcutter advised him to take shelter in his own hut, so the Fox crept in and hid himself in a corner. The huntsman soon came up with his hounds and inquired of the Woodcutter if he had seen the Fox. He declared that he had not seen him, and yet pointed, all the time he was speaking, to the hut where the Fox lay hidden. The huntsman took no notice of the signs, but believing his word, hastened forward in the chase. As soon as they were well away, the Fox departed without taking any notice of the Woodcutter: whereon he called to him and reproached him, saying, "You ungrateful fellow, you owe your life to me, and yet you leave me without a word of thanks." The Fox replied, "Indeed, I should have thanked you **fervently** if your deeds had been as good as your words, and if your hands had not been traitors to your speech."

The Ants And The Grasshopper

6   THE ANTS were spending a fine winter's day drying grain collected in the summertime. A Grasshopper, **perishing** with famine, passed by and earnestly begged for a little food. The Ants inquired of him, "Why did you not treasure up food during the summer?' He replied, "I had not leisure enough. I passed the days in singing." They then said in **derision**: "If you were foolish enough to sing all the summer, you must dance supperless to bed in the winter."

The Wolf In Sheep's Clothing

7   ONCE UPON A TIME a Wolf **resolved** to disguise his appearance in order to secure food more easily. Encased in the skin of a sheep, he pastured with the flock deceiving the shepherd by his costume. In the evening he was shut up by the shepherd in the fold; the gate was closed, and the entrance made thoroughly secure. But the shepherd, returning to the fold during the night to obtain meat for the next day, mistakenly caught up the Wolf instead of a sheep, and killed him instantly.

8   Harm seek. Harm find.

THINK QUESTIONS

1. How are the moral lessons in "The Swollen Fox" and "The Honey Pot" alike? Cite textual evidence in your answer and explain how you got it.

2. Use textual evidence to explain why Aesop might have used animals as characters to teach moral lessons.

3. How are the cottager and his wife in "The Hen and the Golden Eggs" similar to the miser in "The Miser?" What lesson is Aesop teaching in both fables? Cite passages in the text that support your answer.

4. Use context to determine the meaning of the word **deprived** as it is used in the fable "The Hen and the Golden Eggs." Write your definition of "deprived" and tell how you got it. Then, use a dictionary to check your definition.

5. The Latin suffix -*ly*, which means "in what manner," is used in English for many adverbs. Use your knowledge of the suffix and the context clues provided in the passage to determine the meaning of **fervently**. Write your definition of "fervently" and tell how you got it. Then, check your definition in a dictionary. How does your definition differ from the official one?

STUDYSYNC LIBRARY | Aesop's Fables

CLOSE READ

Reread the excerpts from *Aesop's Fables*. As you reread, complete the Focus Questions below. Then use your answers and annotations from the questions to help you complete the Writing Prompt.

FOCUS QUESTIONS

1. Reread "The Ants and the Grasshopper." Highlight the human characteristics that Aesop gives the insects in this fable. What kind of people would these insects be? Make annotations about what Aesop might be trying to express through this personification, and how it supports the fable's moral, or theme.

2. State the message of "The Hen and the Golden Eggs" as a moral, as if you were Aesop and were adding it as a last sentence for the fable. Highlight and cite evidence in the text that points to the moral.

3. Reread "The Miser" and make annotations to explain how placing the stone in the hole helps convey the fable's theme. Use evidence from the text and make annotations noting evidence that supports your thinking.

4. Reread "The Fox and the Woodcutter." Why do you think the author chose to personify a fox in this fable, and what kind of person do you think the fox represents? What does the Fox want the woodcutter to learn from this experience? State your answer in the form of a theme, and cite specific evidence from the text in your answer.

5. The moral of "The Wolf in Sheep's Clothing" is, "Harm seek. Harm find." Explain this moral in your own words. Cite textual evidence in your answer and make annotations that support your explanation of the moral.

WRITING PROMPT

Though written centuries ago, how do the morals and themes of Aesop's fables continue to inspire and inform readers even today? Consider the themes in the fables you have read, along with the thoughts, words, and actions of the characters, and the author's use of personification to support and express themes. Explain how these are still relevant to an audience of readers today. Respond by developing and supporting your ideas with textual evidence from at least three of the fables you have read.

THE LIGHTNING THIEF

FICTION
Rick Riordan
2005

INTRODUCTION

Greek gods come to life in Rick Riordan's fantasy novel, *The Lightning Thief*. After being kicked out of boarding school, again, twelve-year-old Percy Jackson learns that his father is Poseidon, God of the Sea. Before long, Percy and his friends are off on a dangerous mission to find Zeus's missing lightning bolt, which must be returned before Mount Olympus erupts into war. Here, Percy questions his mother about the father who abandoned him, and then reflects on the odd things that seem to happen to him wherever he goes.

"She never exactly said, but I knew why the beach was special to her."

FIRST READ

From Chapter 3

1. Our rental cabin was on the south shore, way out at the tip of Long Island. It was a little pastel box with faded curtains, half sunken into the dunes. There was always sand in the sheets and spiders in the cabinets, and most of the time the sea was too cold to swim in.

2. I loved the place.

3. We'd been going there since I was a baby. My mom had been going even longer. She never exactly said, but I knew why the beach was special to her. It was the place where she'd met my dad.

4. As we got closer to Montauk, she seemed to grow younger, years of worry and work disappearing from her face. Her eyes turned the color of the sea.

5. We got there at sunset, opened all the cabin's windows, and went through our usual cleaning routine. We walked on the beach, fed blue corn chips to the seagulls, and munched on blue jelly beans, blue saltwater taffy, and all the other free samples my mom had brought from work.

6. I guess I should explain about the blue food.

7. See, Gabe had once told my mom there was no such thing. They had this fight, which seemed like a really small thing at the time. But ever since, my mom went out of her way to eat blue. She baked blue birthday cakes. She mixed blueberry smoothies. She bought blue-corn tortilla chips and brought home blue candy from the shop. This—along with keeping her maiden name, Jackson, rather than calling herself Mrs. Ugliano—was proof that she wasn't totally suckered by Gabe. She did have a **rebellious** streak, like me.

8   When it got dark, we made a fire. We roasted hot dogs and marshmallows. Mom told me stories about when she was a kid, back before her parents died in the plane crash. She told me about the books she wanted to write someday, when she had enough money to quit the candy shop.

9   Eventually, I got up the nerve to ask about what was always on my mind whenever we came to Montauk—my father. Mom's eyes went all misty. I figured she would tell me the same things she always did, but I never got tired of hearing them.

10 "He was kind, Percy," she said. "Tall, handsome, and powerful. But gentle, too. You have his black hair, you know, and his green eyes."

11 Mom fished a blue jelly bean out of her candy bag. "I wish he could see you, Percy. He would be so proud."

12 I wondered how she could say that. What was so great about me? A **dyslexic, hyperactive** boy with a D+ report card, kicked out of school for the sixth time in six years.

13 "How old was I?" I asked. "I mean . . . when he left?"

14 She watched the flames. "He was only with me for one summer, Percy. Right here at this beach. This cabin."

15 "But . . . he knew me as a baby."

16 "No, honey. He knew I was expecting a baby, but he never saw you. He had to leave before you were born."

17 I tried to square that with the fact that I seemed to remember . . . something about my father. A warm glow. A smile.

18 I had always assumed he knew me as a baby. My mom had never said it outright, but still, I'd felt it must be true. Now, to be told that he'd never even seen me . . .

19 I felt angry at my father. Maybe it was stupid, but I **resented** him for going on that ocean voyage, for not having the guts to marry my mom. He'd left us, and now we were stuck with Smelly Gabe.

20 "Are you going to send me away again?" I asked her. "To another boarding school?"

21 She pulled a marshmallow from the fire.

22. "I don't know, honey." Her voice was heavy. "I think . . . I think we'll have to do something."

23. "Because you don't want me around?" I regretted the words as soon as they were out.

24. My mom's eyes welled with tears. She took my hand, squeezed it tight. "Oh, Percy, no. I—I have to, honey. For your own good. I have to send you away."

25. Her words reminded me of what Mr. Brunner had said—that it was best for me to leave Yancy.

26. "Because I'm not normal," I said.

27. "You say that as if it's a bad thing, Percy. But you don't realize how important you are. I thought Yancy Academy would be far enough away. I thought you'd finally be safe."

28. "Safe from what?"

29. She met my eyes, and a flood of memories came back to me—all the weird, scary things that had ever happened to me, some of which I'd tried to forget.

30. During third grade, a man in a black trench coat had stalked me on the playground. When the teachers threatened to call the police, he went away growling, but no one believed me when I told them that under his broad-brimmed hat, the man only had one eye, right in the middle of his head.

31. Before that—a really early memory. I was in preschool, and a teacher accidentally put me down for a nap in a cot that a snake had slithered into. My mom screamed when she came to pick me up and found me playing with a limp, scaly rope I'd somehow managed to strangle to death with my meaty toddler hands.

32. In every single school, something creepy had happened, something unsafe, and I was forced to move.

33. I knew I should tell my mom about the old ladies at the fruit stand, and Mrs. Dodds at the art museum, about my weird **hallucination** that I had sliced my math teacher into dust with a sword. But I couldn't make myself tell her. I had a strange feeling the news would end our trip to Montauk, and I didn't want that.

34. "I've tried to keep you as close to me as I could," my mom said. "They told me that was a mistake. But there's only one other option, Percy—the place your

father wanted to send you. And I just . . . I just can't stand to do it."

35. "My father wanted me to go to a special school?"

36. "Not a school," she said softly. "A summer camp."

37. My head was spinning. Why would my dad—who hadn't even stayed around long enough to see me born—talk to my mom about a summer camp? And if it was so important, why hadn't she ever mentioned it before?

38. "I'm sorry, Percy," she said, seeing the look in my eyes. "But I can't talk about it. I—I couldn't send you to that place. It might mean saying good-bye to you for good."

39. "For good? But if it's only a summer camp . . ."

40. She turned toward the fire, and I knew from her expression that if I asked her any more questions she would start to cry.

Excerpted from *The Lightning Thief* by Rick Riordan, published by Miramax Books/Hyperion Books for Children.

 THINK QUESTIONS

1. How does Percy describe himself? Is his view of himself largely positive or negative? Cite textual evidence to support your response.

2. How do Percy's beliefs about why he attends boarding school differ from those of his mother? Use textual evidence to support your response.

3. What does Percy discover about his father? In what way does that cause him to feel conflicted? Support your response with textual evidence.

4. Use context to determine the meaning of the word **rebellious** as it is used in *The Lightning Thief*. Write your definition of "rebellious" and tell how you arrived at it.

5. Remembering that the Greek prefix *dys-* means "difficult" and the Greek root *lex* means "words," use the context clues provided in the passage to determine the meaning of **dyslexic**. Write your definition of "dyslexic" and tell how you arrived at it. Then check your definition against a print or online dictionary and revise it, if necessary.

STUDYSYNC LIBRARY | The Lightning Thief

CLOSE READ

Reread the excerpt from *The Lightening Thief*. As you reread, complete the Focus Questions below. Then use your answers and annotations from the questions to help you complete the Writing Prompt.

FOCUS QUESTIONS

1. In paragraph 7, what can you infer about Percy's mother's relationship with her husband Gabe? What does this tell you about her character? Highlight textual evidence that supports your inference, and make annotations to note specific reasons for it.

2. Look for several examples of information about Percy that are directly stated by the author in paragraph 12. Use these examples, along with Percy's narration, to make an inference about Percy's character. Highlight the textual evidence on which you base your inference, and annotate ideas that explain it.

3. As you reread paragraphs 9–19, analyze how Percy's point of view regarding his father differs from his mother's. Highlight specific textual evidence from the paragraphs that helps you contrast the two points of view, and annotate your ideas on why the differences exist.

4. Paragraph 31 describes how as a preschooler, Percy strangles a snake in his cot. This scene alludes, or refers, to the Greek hero Hercules, who is famed for doing the same thing. Hercules, who is half human and half god, is also known for his great strength and the completion of a series of 12 seemingly impossible labors or tasks. Highlight evidence from the text that refers to this allusion, and make annotations to note what the information about Hercules helps you infer about Percy.

5. Closely read the last seven paragraphs. What inferences are you able to make about the "summer camp" that Percy's dad wants to send Percy to? Highlight textual evidence and annotate ideas that support your response.

WRITING PROMPT

Because *The Lightning Thief* is told from Percy's first-person point of view, the reader starts out just as much in the dark about what might be happening in his life as he is. Write an essay that analyzes how that fact affects the way readers experience the story. How does this point of view build drama and suspense? How do inferences help the reader gain an understanding of events that even Percy might not have? Support your analysis with textual evidence.

PERSEUS

POETRY
Robert Hayden
1966

INTRODUCTION

Widely acclaimed for his poetry about the black historical experience, Robert Hayden was the first African American to serve as Consultant in Poetry to the Library of Congress. Here, Hayden offers a new perspective on the Greek mythical hero Perseus. Gazing down on the severed head of Medusa, the snake-haired Gorgon, Perseus has a moment of self-reflection, and acknowledges his powerful and dangerous "thirst . . . to destroy."

STUDYSYNC LIBRARY | Perseus

"I struck. The shield flashed bare."

FIRST READ

1. Her sleeping head with its great **gelid** mass
2. of serpents **torpidly** astir
3. burned into the mirroring shield—
4. a **scathing** image cire
5. as hated truth the mind accepts at last
6. and **festers** on.
7. I struck. The shield flashed bare.

8. Yet even as I lifted up the head
9. and started from that place
10. of gazing silences and terrored stone,
11. I thirsted to destroy.
12. None could have passed me then—
13. no garland-bearing girl, no priest
14. or staring boy—and lived.

"Perseus". Copyright © 1966 by Robert Hayden, from COLLECTED POEMS OF ROBERT HAYDEN by Robert Hayden, edited by Frederick Glaysher. Copyright © 1985 by Emma Hayden. Used by permission of Liveright Publishing Corporation.

THINK QUESTIONS

1. What does line 10 tell you about the setting of Medusa's resting place? Explain using evidence from the text to support your answer.

2. How is Perseus able to behead the snake-haired Medusa without turning to "terrored stone"? Cite textual evidence to support your answer.

3. After Perseus kills Medusa, what "hated truth" does he acknowledge about himself? Cite textual evidence to support your answer.

4. The word **gelid** is used in line 1 to describe the serpents on Medusa's head. What meaning of "gelid" would you infer from lines 1 and 2? Write your definition of "gelid" and tell how you arrived at it. Then, check your meaning against a print or online dictionary and revise if necessary.

5. Use context to infer the meaning of the word **torpidly** as it is used in "Perseus." Write your definition of "torpidly" here and state the clue(s) from the text you used to determine the meaning.

STUDYSYNC LIBRARY | Perseus

CLOSE READ

Reread the poem "Perseus." As you reread, complete the Focus Questions below. Then use your answers and annotations from the questions to help you complete the Writing Prompt.

FOCUS QUESTIONS

1. Use context clues to define the word **mass** as it is used in line 1 of the poem. Highlight the context clues and annotate to write your definition of the word and explore its connotations, or emotional connections. Then, analyze why the poet uses this word rather than a synonym. Support your ideas with evidence from the text.

2. What do you notice about the structure of the sentences that make up the first stanza? Highlight textual evidence and make annotations to help you explain how this structure impacts the tone this portion of the poem conveys.

3. Explain the poet's use of the phrase "gazing silences" in line 10. Cite textual evidence by highlighting clues that explain its meaning, and make annotations to explore the connotations of the words. (You may wish to use a dictionary or thesaurus to compare the connotations of some of the synonyms.) Support your ideas about why the phrase is effective with evidence from the poem.

4. How do the examples Perseus provides in lines 13 and 14 impact the meaning of what he is telling his audience at the end of the poem? How do they fit in with the poem's tone? Highlight specific examples of words and phrases, and make annotations to support your thinking. Cite textual evidence to support your ideas.

5. How do Perseus's actions call into question the qualities one historically associates with the idea of a hero? What lessons can be learned from Perseus's actions? How do they inform us? Support your ideas with textual evidence.

WRITING PROMPT

More than anything, "Perseus" shares with readers the inner struggle of a hero who finds that he is perhaps more like his bloodthirsty enemy than he realized. Trace the tone conveyed throughout the poem. How does the tone of the poem help readers better understand Perseus's conflict? How does the poet's choice of words and phrases, in both their denotative and connotative meanings, support this tone and help readers compare and contrast both sides of a hero? Support your writing with specific examples from the text.

HEROES EVERY CHILD SHOULD KNOW: PERSEUS

FICTION
Hamilton Wright Mabie
1914

INTRODUCTION

Perseus, the son of a mortal woman, Danaë, and Zeus, the king of the gods, faced challenges from the day he was born. Locked in a wooden chest, the infant and his mother were set adrift in the sea. They washed up safely on a remote island, where a fisherman took them in. Eventually, Perseus grew into a fine, able-bodied young man. One fateful day, he was visited by the goddess Athena, who had chosen him for the task of killing her bitter enemy Medusa, the snake-haired Gorgon whose gaze would turn a beholder to stone. Perseus was all too willing to take on the mission, even if it meant dying in the process.

"I will go, though I die in going."

FIRST READ

From Chapter I: Perseus

1 Then Athene smiled and said:

2 "Be patient, and listen; for if you forget my words, you will indeed die. You must go northward to the country of the Hyperboreans, who live beyond the pole, at the sources of the cold north wind, till you find the three Grey Sisters, who have but one eye and one tooth between them. You must ask them the way to the Nymphs, the daughters of the Evening Star, who dance about the golden tree, in the Atlantic island of the west. They will tell you the way to the Gorgon, that you may slay her, my enemy, the mother of monstrous beasts. Once she was a maiden as beautiful as morn, till in her pride she sinned a sin at which the sun hid his face; and from that day her hair was turned to vipers, and her hands to eagle's claws; and her heart was filled with shame and rage, and her lips with bitter venom; and her eyes became so terrible that whosoever looks on them is turned to stone; and her children are the winged horse and the giant of the golden sword; and her grandchildren are Echidna the witch-adder, and Geryon the three-headed tyrant, who feeds his herds beside the herds of hell. So she became the sister of the Gorgons, the daughters of the Queen of the Sea. Touch them not, for they are **immortal;** but bring me only Medusa's head."

3 "And I will bring it!" said Perseus; "but how am I to escape her eyes? Will she not freeze me too into stone?"

4 "You shall take this polished shield," said Athene, "and when you come near her look not at her yourself, but at her image in the brass; so you may strike her safely. And when you have struck off her head, wrap it, with your face turned away, in the folds of the goatskin on which the shield hangs. So you will bring it safely back to me, and win to yourself **renown,** and a place among the heroes who feast with the Immortals upon the peak where no winds blow."

5. Then Perseus said, "I will go, though I die in going. But how shall I cross the seas without a ship? And who will show me my way? And when I find her, how shall I slay her, if her scales be iron and brass?"

6. Now beside Athene appeared a young man more light-limbed than the stag, whose eyes were like sparks of fire. By his side was a **scimitar** of diamond, all of one clear precious stone, and on his feet were golden sandals, from the heels of which grew living wings.

7. Then the young man spoke: "These sandals of mine will bear you across the seas, and over hill and dale like a bird, as they bear me all day long; for I am Hermes, the far-famed Argus-slayer, the messenger of the Immortals who dwell on Olympus."

8. Then Perseus fell down and worshipped, while the young man spoke again:

9. "The sandals themselves will guide you on the road, for they are divine and cannot stray; and this sword itself the Argus-slayer, will kill her, for it is divine, and needs no second stroke. Arise, and gird them on, and go forth."

10. So Perseus arose, and girded on the sandals and the sword.

11. And Athene cried, "Now leap from the cliff and be gone."

12. But Perseus lingered.

13. "May I not bid farewell to my mother and to Dictys? And may I not offer burnt offerings to you, and to Hermes the far-famed Argus-slayer, and to Father Zeus above?"

14. "You shall not bid farewell to your mother, lest your heart **relent** at her weeping. I will comfort her and Dictys until you return in peace. Nor shall you offer burnt offerings to the Olympians; for your offering shall be Medusa's head. Leap, and trust in the armour of the Immortals."

15. Then Perseus looked down the cliff and shuddered; but he was ashamed to show his dread. Then he thought of Medusa and the renown before him, and he leapt into the empty air.

16. And behold, instead of falling he floated, and stood, and ran along the sky. He looked back, but Athene had vanished, and Hermes; and the sandals led him on northward ever, like a crane who follows the spring toward the Ister fens.

17. So Perseus started on his journey, going dry-shod over land and sea; and his heart was high and joyful, for the winged sandals bore him each day a seven days' journey. And he turned neither to the right hand nor the left, till he came to the Unshapen Land, and the place which has no name.

18. And seven days he walked through it on a path which few can tell, till he came to the edge of the everlasting night, where the air was full of feathers, and the soil was hard with ice; and there at last he found the three Grey Sisters, by the shore of the freezing sea, nodding upon a white log of driftwood, beneath the cold white winter moon; and they chanted a low song together, "Why the old times were better than the new."

19. There was no living thing around them, not a fly, not a moss upon the rocks. Neither seal nor sea gull dare come near, lest the ice should clutch them in its claws. The surge broke up in foam, but it fell again in flakes of snow; and it frosted the hair of the three Grey Sisters, and the bones in the ice cliff above their heads. They passed the eye from one to the other, but for all that they could not see; and they passed the tooth from one to the other, but for all that they could not eat; and they sat in the full glare of the moon, but they were none the warmer for her beams. And Perseus pitied the three Grey Sisters; but they did not pity themselves.

20. So he said, "Oh, venerable mothers, wisdom is the daughter of old age. You therefore should know many things. Tell me, if you can, the path to the Gorgon."

21. Then one cried, "Who is this who **reproaches** us with old age?" And another, "This is the voice of one of the children of men."

22. Then one cried, "Give me the eye, that I may see him"; and another, "Give me the tooth, that I may bite him." But Perseus, when he saw that they were foolish and proud, and did not love the children of men, left off pitying them. Then he stepped close to them, and watched till they passed the eye from hand to hand. And as they groped about between themselves, he held out his own hand gently, till one of them put the eye into it, fancying that it was the hand of her sister. Then he sprang back, and laughed, and cried:

23. "Cruel and proud old women, I have your eye; and I will throw it into the sea, unless you tell me the path to the Gorgon, and swear to me that you tell me right."

24. Then they wept, and chattered, and scolded; but in vain. They were forced to tell the truth, though, when they told it, Perseus could hardly make out the road.

25. "You must go," they said, "foolish boy, to the southward, into the ugly glare of the sun, till you come to Atlas the Giant, who holds the heaven and the earth apart. And you must ask his daughters, the Hesperides, who are young and foolish like yourself. And now give us back our eye, for we have forgotten all the rest."

STUDYSYNC LIBRARY | Heroes Every Child Should Know: Perseus

26 So Perseus gave them back their eye. And he leaped away to the southward, leaving the snow and the ice behind. And the terns and the sea gulls swept laughing round his head, and called to him to stop and play, and the dolphins gambolled up as he passed, and offered to carry him on their back. And all night long the sea nymphs sang sweetly. Day by day the sun rose higher and leaped more swiftly into the sea at night, and more swiftly out of the sea at dawn; while Perseus skimmed over the billows like a sea gull, and his feet were never wetted; and leapt on from wave to wave, and his limbs were never weary, till he saw far away a mighty mountain, all rose-red in the setting sun. Perseus knew that it was Atlas, who holds the heavens and the earth apart.

27 He leapt on shore, and wandered upward, among pleasant valleys and waterfalls. At last he heard sweet voices singing; and he guessed that he was come to the garden of the Nymphs, the daughters of the Evening Star. They sang like nightingales among the thickets, and Perseus stopped to hear their song; but the words which they spoke he could not understand. So he stepped forward and saw them dancing, hand in hand around the charmed tree, which bent under its golden fruit; and round the tree foot was coiled the dragon, old Ladon the sleepless snake, who lies there for ever, listening to the song of the maidens, blinking and watching with dry bright eyes.

28 Then Perseus stopped, not because he feared the dragon, but because he was bashful before those fair maids; but when they saw him, they too stopped, and called to him with trembling voices:

29 "Who are you, fair boy? Come dance with us around the tree in the garden which knows no winter, the home of the south wind and the sun. Come hither and play with us awhile; we have danced alone here for a thousand years, and our hearts are weary with longing for a playfellow."

30 "I cannot dance with you, fair maidens; for I must do the errand of the Immortals. So tell me the way to the Gorgon, lest I wander and perish in the waves."

31 Then they sighed and wept; and answered:

32 "The Gorgon! she will freeze you into stone."

33 "It is better to die like a hero than to live like an ox in a stall. The Immortals have lent me weapons, and they will give me wit to use them."

34 Then they sighed again and answered: "Fair boy, if you are bent on your own ruin, be it so. We know not the way to the Gorgon; but we will ask the giant Atlas above upon the mountain peak." So they went up the mountain to Atlas their uncle, and Perseus went up with them. And they found the giant kneeling, as he held the heavens and the earth apart.

35. They asked him, and he answered mildly, pointing to the sea board with his mighty hand, "I can see the Gorgons lying on an island far away, but this youth can never come near them, unless he has the hat of darkness, which whosoever wears cannot be seen."

36. Then cried Perseus, "Where is that hat, that I may find it?"

37. But the giant smiled. "No living mortal can find that hat, for it lies in the depths of Hades, in the regions of the dead. But my nieces are immortal, and they shall fetch it for you, if you will promise me one thing and keep your faith."

38. Then Perseus promised; and the giant said, "When you come back with the head of Medusa, you shall show me the beautiful horror, that I may lose my feeling and my breathing, and become a stone for ever; for it is weary labour for me to hold the heavens and the earth apart."

39. Then Perseus promised, and the eldest of the Nymphs went down, and into a dark cavern among the cliffs, out of which came smoke and thunder, for it was one of the mouths of hell.

40. And Perseus and the Nymphs sat down seven days and waited trembling, till the Nymph came up again; and her face was pale, and her eyes dazzled with the light for she had been long in the dreary darkness; but in her hand was the magic hat.

41. Then all the Nymphs kissed Perseus, and wept over him a long while; but he was only impatient to be gone. And at last they put the hat upon his head, and he vanished out of their sight.

42. But Perseus went on boldly, past many an ugly sight, far away into the heart of the Unshapen Land, till he heard the rustle of the Gorgons' wings and saw the glitter of their **brazen** talons; and then he knew that it was time to halt, lest Medusa should freeze him into stone.

43. He thought awhile with himself, and remembered Athene's words. He arose aloft into the air, and held the mirror of the shield above his head, and looked up into it that he might see all that was below him.

44. And he saw the three Gorgons sleeping. He knew that they could not see him, because the hat of darkness hid him; and yet he trembled as he sank down near them, so terrible were those brazen claws.

45. Two of the Gorgons were foul as swine, and lay sleeping heavily, with their mighty wings outspread; but Medusa tossed to and fro restlessly, and as she tossed Perseus pitied her. But as he looked, from among her tresses the vipers' heads awoke, and peeped up with their bright dry eyes, and showed

their fangs, and hissed; and Medusa, as she tossed, threw back her wings and showed her brazen claws.

46. Then Perseus came down and stepped to her boldly, and looked steadfastly on his mirror, and struck with Herpe stoutly once; and he did not need to strike again.

47. Then he wrapped the head in the goat-skin, turning away his eyes, and sprang into the air aloft, faster than he ever sprang before.

48. For Medusa's wings and talons rattled as she sank dead upon the rocks; and her two foul sisters woke, and saw her lying dead.

49. Into the air they sprang yelling, and looked for him who had done the deed. They rushed, sweeping and flapping, like eagles after a hare; and Perseus's blood ran cold as he saw them come howling on his track; and he cried, "Bear me well now, brave sandals, for the hounds of Death are at my heels!"

50. And well the brave sandals bore him, aloft through cloud and sunshine, across the shoreless sea; and fast followed the hounds of Death. But the sandals were too swift, even for Gorgons, and by nightfall they were far behind, two black specks in the southern sky, till the sun sank and he saw them no more.

THINK QUESTIONS

1. Refer to one or more details from the text to explain what Athene asks Perseus to do and how Athene and Hermes equip Perseus for the task.

2. Citing evidence from the text, write two or three sentences explaining how Perseus continues to receive help from others in the accomplishment of his quest.

3. Cite textual evidence to describe how Perseus feels when he first gazes on the sleeping Medusa, as well as how and why these feelings change.

4. Use context clues to determine the meaning of the word **renown** as it is used in *Heroes Every Child Should Know: Perseus*. Write your definition of "renown" and tell how you arrived at it. Then, use a thesaurus or other reference book to identify at least one synonym for "renown." How do these synonyms help clarify the word's meaning?

5. The Latin prefix *in-* means "not," the root *mort* means "death," and the suffix *-al* means "characterized by." Use these root and affix meanings, along with context clues provided in the passage, to determine the meaning of **immortal.** Write your definition of "immortal" and tell how you got it.

STUDYSYNC LIBRARY | Heroes Every Child Should Know: Perseus

 CLOSE READ

Reread the excerpt from *Heroes Every Child Should Know: Perseus*. As you reread, complete the Focus Questions below. Then use your answers and annotations from the questions to help you complete the Writing Prompt.

 FOCUS QUESTIONS

1. Summarize the scene between Perseus, Atlas, and his nieces (paragraphs 27–41). Why is it important to the development of the plot? Identify specific phrases or sentences that play an important role in the overall plot. Support your response with specific evidence from the text.

2. Paragraph 45 uses the word **brazen** to describe Medusa's claws. Another definition of *brazen* is "without shame." How does this other definition apply to Medusa? Does it help justify Perseus's actions against Medusa? Discuss the multiple meanings of the word "brazen" as it is used here, and cite specific evidence from the text in your response.

3. In what ways does Perseus's ultimate escape from the Gorgons resolve the story's conflict? Highlight textual evidence and make annotations noting ideas that help you evaluate the closure the resolution provides.

4. How do the ideas of being mortal or immortal affect the plot of the myth? Discuss the meanings of these words and make annotations to trace the development of these ideas in the story. Cite specific evidence from the text in your response.

5. How is the plot of the myth of Perseus similar to and different from that of the narrative poem "Perseus"? Highlight specific evidence from both texts that helps you compare and contrast them, and annotate to explain why those words or phrases show the similarities and differences of the two plots.

WRITING PROMPT

Compare and contrast how the shared plot events in the poem "Perseus" and the myth *Heroes Every Child Should Know: Perseus* affect the character of Perseus, as well as how he changes as a result. In your response, analyze what Perseus learns about himself in each text, along with how that realization impacts the resolution shared with readers. Remember to support your writing with evidence from the text.

BLACK SHIPS BEFORE TROY: THE STORY OF THE ILIAD

FICTION
Rosemary Sutcliff
1993

INTRODUCTION

The ancient Greeks and Trojans fought for 10 long years over Helen, but why? What forces brought Paris, a Trojan prince, and Helen, the most beautiful women in the world, together in the first place? Author Rosemary Sutcliffe's book tells the story of the Trojan War, which had its origins in a golden apple presented to the "fairest" of the goddesses.

"All she did—it seemed a small thing—was to toss down on the table a golden apple."

 **FIRST READ**

Excerpt From "The Golden Apple"

1   In the high and far-off days when men were heroes and walked with the gods, Peleus, king of the Myrmidons, took for his wife a sea **nymph** called Thetis, Thetis of the Silver Feet. Many guests came to their wedding feast, and among the mortal guests came all the gods of high Olympus.

2   But as they sat feasting, one who had not been invited was suddenly in their midst: Eris, the goddess of **discord,** had been left out because wherever she went she took trouble with her; yet here she was, all the same, and in her blackest mood, to **avenge** the insult.

3   All she did—it seemed a small thing—was to toss down on the table a golden apple. Then she breathed upon the guests once, and vanished.

4   The apple lay gleaming among the piled fruits and the brimming wine cups; and bending close to look at it, everyone could see the words "To the fairest" traced on its side.

5   Then the three greatest of the goddesses each claimed that it was hers. Hera claimed it as wife to Zeus, the All-father, and queen of all the gods. Athene claimed that she had the better right, for the beauty of wisdom such as hers surpassed all else. Aphrodite only smiled, and asked who had a better claim to beauty's prize than the goddess of beauty herself.

6   They fell to arguing among themselves; the argument became a quarrel, and the quarrel grew more and more bitter, and each called upon the assembled guests to judge between them. But the other guests refused, for they knew well enough that whichever goddess they chose to receive the golden apple, they would make enemies of the other two.

7 In the end, the three took the quarrel home with them to Olympus. The other gods took sides, some with one and some with another, and the ill will between them dragged on for a long while. More than long enough, in the world of men, for a child born when the quarrel first began to grow to manhood and become a warrior or a herdsman. But the immortal gods do not know time as mortals know it.

8 Now on the northeast coast of the Aegean Sea, there was a city of men. Troy was its name, a great city surrounded by strong walls, and standing on a hill hard by the shore. It had grown rich on the tolls that its kings demanded from merchant ships passing up the nearby straits to the Black Sea cornlands and down again. Priam, who was now king, was lord of wide realms and long-maned horses, and he had many sons about his hearth. And when the quarrel about the golden apple was still raw and new, a last son was born to him and his wife Queen Hecuba, and they called him Paris.

9 There should have been great rejoicing, but while Hecuba still carried the babe within her, the **soothsayers** had foretold that she would give birth to a firebrand that should burn down Troy. And so, when he was born and named, the king bade a servant carry him out into the wilderness and leave him to die. The servant did as he was bid; but a herdsman searching for a missing calf found the babe and brought him up as his own.

10 The boy grew tall and strong and beautiful, the swiftest runner and the best archer in all the country around. So his boyhood passed among the oak woods and the high hill-pastures that rose toward Mount Ida. And there he met and fell in love with wood nymph called Oenone, who loved him in return. She had the gift of being able to heal the wounds of mortal men, no matter how sorely they were hurt.

11 Among the oak woods they lived together and were happy—until one day the three jealous goddesses, still quarreling about the golden apple, chanced to look down from Olympus, and saw the beautiful young man herding his cattle on the slopes of Mount Ida. They knew, for the gods know all things, that he was the son of Priam, king of Troy, though he himself did not know it yet; but the thought came to them that he would not know who they were, and therefore he would not be afraid to judge between them. They were growing somewhat weary of the argument by then.

12 So they tossed the apple down to him, and Paris put up his hands and caught it. After it the three came down, landing before him so lightly that their feet did not bend the mountain grasses, and bade him choose between them, which was the fairest and had best right to the prize he held in his hand.

13 First Athene, in her gleaming armor, fixed him with sword-gray eyes and promised him supreme wisdom if he would name her.

14 Then Hera, in her royal robes as queen of heaven, promised him **vast** wealth and power and honour, if he awarded her the prize.

15 Lastly, Aphrodite drew near, her eyes as blue as deep-sea water, her hair like spun gold wreathed around her head, and, smiling honey-sweet, whispered that she would give him a wife as fair as herself, if he tossed the apple to her.

16 And Paris forgot the other two with their offers of wisdom and power, forgot also, for that moment, dark-haired Oenone in the shadowed oak woods; and he gave the golden apple to Aphrodite.

17 Then Athene and Hera were angry with him for refusing them the prize, just as the wedding guests had known that they would be; and both of them were angry with Aphrodite. But Aphrodite was well content, and set about keeping her promise to the herdsman who was a king's son.

Excerpted from *Black Ships Before Troy* by Rosemary Sutcliff, published by Frances Lincoln Children's Books.

THINK QUESTIONS

1. How did the argument about which goddess was the "fairest" begin? Support your answer with evidence from the text.

2. Why did the goddesses consider Paris a good choice to judge the contest between them? Cite textual evidence that supports your answer.

3. What does Paris's choice for the winner of the contest help you infer about him? Indicate the textual evidence you used to make your inference.

4. Use context to determine the meaning of the word **nymph** as it is used in *Black Ships Before Troy*. Write your definition of "nymph" and tell how you arrived at it.

5. The Latin affix *dis-* means "away" or "apart," and the root *cord* means "heart." Use these meanings, along with context clues, to determine the meaning of the word **discord** as it is used in *Black Ships Before Troy*. Write your definition of "discord" and tell how you got it.

STUDYSYNC LIBRARY | Black Ships Before Troy: The Story of the Iliad

CLOSE READ

Reread the excerpt from *Black Ships Before Troy*. As you reread, complete the Focus Questions below. Then use your answers and annotations from the questions to help you complete the Writing Prompt.

FOCUS QUESTIONS

1. Paragraph 2 introduces Eris, the goddess of discord. In what way does her title help you understand her actions? Highlight evidence from the text that indicates the motive, or reason, she has for behaving that way. Then use textual evidence from paragraphs 4 and 5 to analyze why she challenges the goddesses to what is essentially a beauty contest. Highlight details and make annotations that support your thinking.

2. In paragraph 7, the narrative pauses to describe the actions of the Greek gods on Olympus. What information is conveyed here, and why is this section important to the story? Highlight relevant evidence from the text and make annotations to explain what the information indicates.

3. Foreshadowing, or hinting at an event that may happen further on in a story, is a plot device often used to structure a story. Paragraph 7 states that in the time the gods spent quarreling about the goddesses and the golden apple, a child could have grown up and "become a warrior or a herdsman." Highlight textual evidence in paragraphs 8 and 9 that indicate that the statement foreshadows something about Paris's life. Make annotations to explain your ideas.

4. Readers of *Black Ships Before Troy* could likely follow the plot of the story without the mention of Oenone in paragraph 10. What does knowledge of her presence add to your understanding of Paris and his actions in the final paragraphs of the myth? Annotate ideas and highlight relevant evidence from the text to support your answer.

5. Compare and contrast how the goddess Athene is presented in the selections *Black Ships Before Troy* and *Heroes Every Child Should Know: Perseus*. From both texts, what can you infer about this goddess? Annotate ideas and highlight relevant evidence from both texts to support your answer.

WRITING PROMPT

Black Ships Before Troy is essentially a series of three events: a wedding between a goddess and a mortal, a challenge that an envious goddess poses to three more powerful goddesses, and a judgment made by a mortal prince/herdsman. Analyze how the structure of the text helps connect and develop these three events. How does one event inform the other? In your analysis, give examples of how specific parts of the text connect and contribute to the development of the plot. Remember to support your ideas with textual evidence throughout your writing.

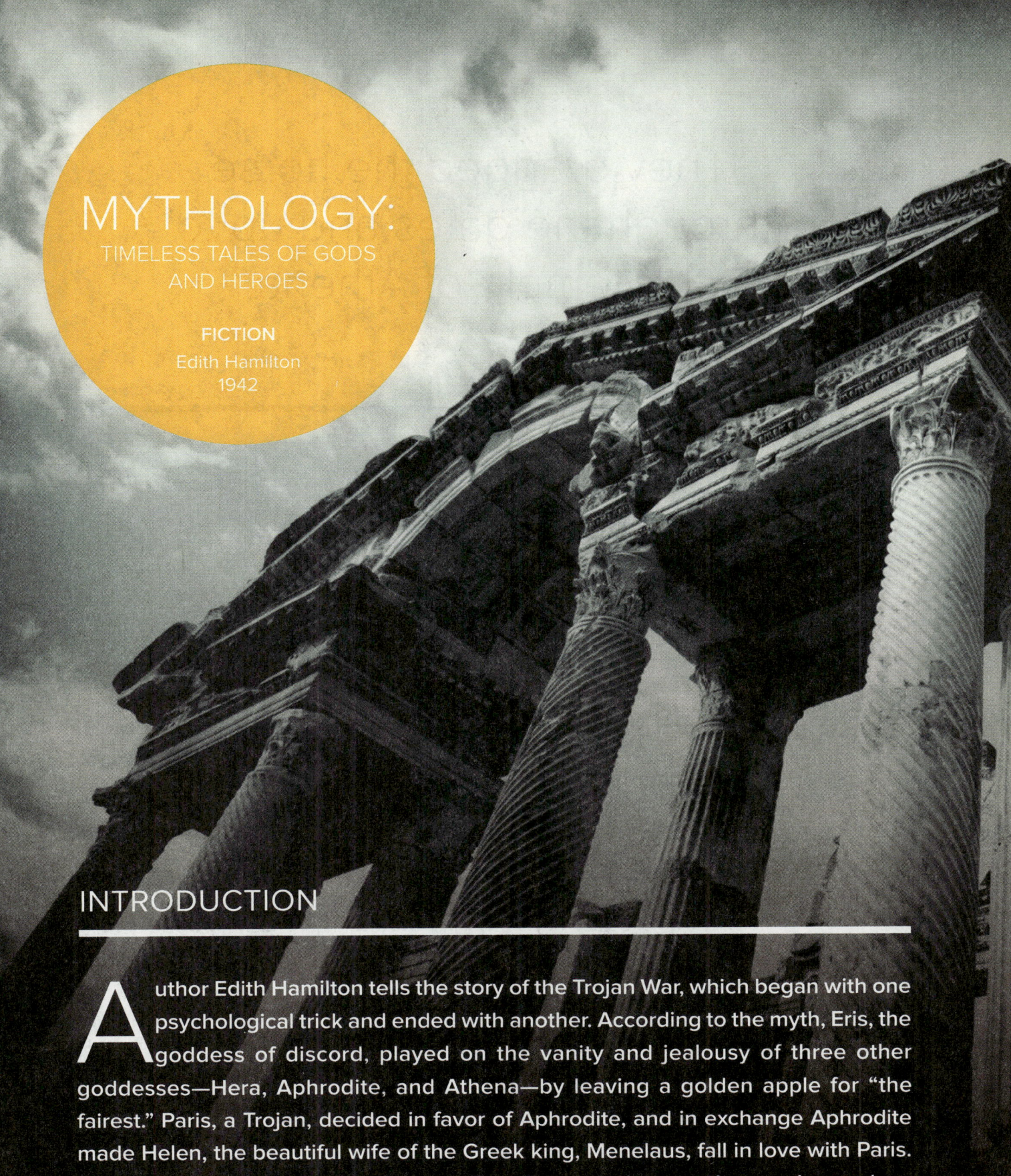

MYTHOLOGY:
TIMELESS TALES OF GODS AND HEROES

FICTION
Edith Hamilton
1942

INTRODUCTION

Author Edith Hamilton tells the story of the Trojan War, which began with one psychological trick and ended with another. According to the myth, Eris, the goddess of discord, played on the vanity and jealousy of three other goddesses—Hera, Aphrodite, and Athena—by leaving a golden apple for "the fairest." Paris, a Trojan, decided in favor of Aphrodite, and in exchange Aphrodite made Helen, the beautiful wife of the Greek king, Menelaus, fall in love with Paris. Outraged, the Greeks declared war on Troy. Ten years later, as the war dragged on,

"They dragged the horse through the gates and up to the temple of Athena."

FIRST READ

From Part Four, Chapter Two: The Fall of Troy

1. [The Greeks] saw clearly by now that unless they could get their Army into the city and take the Trojans by surprise, they would never conquer. Almost ten years had passed since they had first laid siege to the town, and it seemed as strong as ever. The walls stood uninjured. They had never suffered a real attack. The fighting had taken place, for the most part, at a distance from them. The Greeks must find a secret way of entering the city, or accept defeat. The result of this new determination and new vision was the stratagem of the wooden horse. It was, as anyone would guess, the creation of Odysseus' wily mind.

2. He had a skillful worker in wood make a huge wooden horse which was hollow and so big that it could hold a number of men. Then he persuaded—and had a great deal of difficulty in doing so—certain of the chieftains to hide inside it, along with himself, of course. They were all terror-stricken except Achilles' son Neoptolemus, and indeed what they faced was no slight danger. The idea was that all the other Greeks should strike camp, and apparently put out to sea, but they would really hide beyond the nearest island where they could not be seen by the Trojans. Whatever happened they would be safe; they could sail home if anything went wrong. But in that case the men inside the wooden horse would surely die.

3. Odysseus, as can be readily believed, had not overlooked this fact. His plan was to leave a single Greek behind in the deserted camp, primed with a tale calculated to make the Trojans draw the horse into the city—and without investigating it. Then, when night was darkest, the Greeks inside were to leave their wooden prison and open the city gates to the Army, which by that time would have sailed back, and be waiting before the wall.

4 A night came when the plan was carried out. Then the last day of Troy dawned. On the wall the Trojan watchers saw with astonishment two sights, each as startling as the other. In front of the Scaean gates stood an enormous figure of a horse, such a thing as no one had ever seen, an **apparition** so strange that it was vaguely terrifying, even though there was no sound or movement coming from it. No sound or movement anywhere, indeed. The noisy Greek camp was hushed; nothing was stirring there. And the ships were gone. Only one conclusion seemed possible: The Greeks had given up. They had sailed for Greece; they had accepted defeat. All Troy **exulted.** Her long warfare was over; her sufferings lay behind her.

5 The people flocked to the abandoned Greek camp to see the sights: here Achilles had sulked so long; there Agamemnon's tent had stood; this was the quarters of the trickster, Odysseus. What rapture to see the places empty, nothing in them now to fear. At last they drifted back to where that monstrosity, the wooden horse, stood, and they gathered around it, puzzled what to do with it. Then the Greek who had been left behind in the camp discovered himself to them. His name was Sinon, and he was a most plausible speaker. He was seized and dragged to Priam, weeping and protesting that he no longer wished to be a Greek. The story he told was one of Odysseus' masterpieces. Pallas Athena had been exceedingly angry, Sinon said, at the theft of the Palladium, and the Greeks in terror had sent to the oracle to ask how they could appease her. The oracle answered: "With blood and with a maiden slain you calmed the winds when first you came to Troy. With blood must your return be sought. With a Greek life make expiation." He himself, Sinon told Priam, was the wretched victim chosen to be sacrificed. All was ready for the awful rite, which was to be carried out just before the Greeks' departure, but in the night he had managed to escape and hidden in a swamp had watched the ships sail away.

6 It was a good tale and the Trojans never questioned it. They pitied Sinon and assured him that he should **henceforth** live as one of themselves. So it befell that by false cunning and pretended tears those were conquered whom great Diomedes had never overcome, nor savage Achilles, nor ten years of warfare, nor a thousand ships. For Sinon did not forget the second part of his story. The wooden horse had been made, he said, as a votive offering to Athena, and the reason for its immense size was to discourage the Trojans from taking it into the city. What the Greeks hoped for was that the Trojans would destroy it and so draw down upon them Athena's anger. Placed in the city, it would turn her favor to them and away from the Greeks. The story was clever enough to have had by itself, in all probability, the desired effect but Poseidon, the most bitter of all the gods against Troy, contrived an addition which made the issue certain. The priest Laocoön, when the horse was first discovered, had been urgent with the Trojans to destroy it. "I fear the Greeks even when they bear gifts," he said. Cassandra, Priam's daughter, had echoed

his warning, but no one ever listened to her and she had gone back to the palace before Sinon appeared. Laocoön and his two sons heard his story with suspicion, the only doubters there. As Sinon finished, suddenly over the sea came two fearful serpents swimming to the land. Once there, they glided straight to Laocoön. They wrapped their huge coils around him and the two lads and they crushed the life out of them. Then they disappeared within Athena's temple.

7 There could be no further hesitation. To the horrified spectators Laocoön had been punished for opposing the entry of the horse which most certainly no one else would now do. All the people cried,

8 "Bring the carven image in.
Bear it to Athena,
Fit gift for the child of Zeus."

9 Who of the young but hurried forth?
Who of the old would stay at home?
With song and rejoicing they brought death in,
Treachery and destruction.

10 They dragged the horse through the gates and up to the temple of Athena. Then, rejoicing in their good fortune, believing the war ended and Athena's favor restored to them, they went to their houses in peace as they had not for ten years.

11 In the middle of the night the door in the horse opened. One by one the chieftains let themselves down. They stole to the gates and threw them wide, and into the sleeping town marched the Greek Army. What they had first to do could be carried out silently. Fires were started in buildings throughout the city. By the time the Trojans were awake, before they realized what had happened, while they were struggling into their armor, Troy was burning. They rushed out to the street one by one in confusion. Bands of soldiers were waiting there to strike each man down before he could join himself to others. It was not fighting, it was butchery. Very many died without ever a chance of dealing a blow in return. In the more distant parts of the town the Trojans were able to gather together here and there and then it was the Greeks who suffered. They were borne down by desperate men who wanted only to kill before they were killed. They knew that the one safety for the conquered was to hope for no safety. This spirit often turned the victors into the **vanquished.** The quickest-witted Trojans tore off their own armor and put on that of the dead Greeks, and many a Greek thinking he was joining friends discovered too late that they were enemies and paid for his error with his life. On top of the houses they tore up the roofs and hurled the beams down upon the Greeks. An entire tower standing on the roof of Priam's palace was

lifted from its foundations and toppled over. Exulting the defenders saw it fall and **annihilate** a great band who were forcing the palace doors. But the success brought only a short respite.

Excerpted from *Mythology: Timeless Tales of Gods and Heroes* by Edith Hamilton, published by Grand Central Publishing.

THINK QUESTIONS

1. What did the Greeks rely on more to defeat the Trojans—cleverness or power? Explain, citing evidence from the text to support your choice.

2. Using textual evidence, write two or three sentences that explain why Odysseus found it difficult to persuade the Greek chieftains to go along with his plan.

3. What were the two parts of Sinon's lie to the Trojans, and why was each part important? Cite textual evidence in your answer.

4. Use context clues to determine the meaning of the word **exulted** as it is used in *Mythology: Timeless Tales of Gods and Heroes*. Write your definition of "exulted" and tell how you arrived at it. Then, use a dictionary to determine the precise part of speech and pronunciation of "exulted" and write what you found.

5. Remembering that the Latin suffix *-tion* means "the state or condition of" and the Latin root *apparare* means "to appear," use the context clues provided in the passage to determine the meaning of **apparition.** Write your definition of "apparition" and tell how you arrived at it.

STUDYSYNC LIBRARY | Mythology: Timeless Tales of Gods and Heroes

CLOSE READ

Reread the excerpt from *Mythology: Timeless Tales of Gods and Heroes*. As you reread, complete the Focus Questions below. Then use your answers and annotations from the questions to help you complete the Writing Prompt.

FOCUS QUESTIONS

1. In the first paragraph on page 39, the author describes the city of Troy, the main setting of this excerpt. How does this description compare to the description of Troy in *Black Ships Before Troy*? Cite textual evidence showing that the setting of the two stories is the same.

2. At the end of the first paragraph of the excerpt, we learn that the idea for the Trojan horse was "the creation of Odysseus' wily mind." How does this sentence convey the meaning of the word "wily"? What other evidence in the passage can you find that support Odysseus being described this way? Highlight text and make annotations to support your response.

3. The tale that Sinon tells includes a reference to winning the support of Athene by bringing the horse into Troy. How does this detail affect the Greeks' decision? What does this tell you about the relationship between mortals and gods at this time, and how does their relationship compare to that portrayed in *Black Ships Before Troy*? Cite textual evidence from both excerpts to support your response.

4. The next-to-last paragraph of the text is very short, but it is important to the development of the plot. How does this paragraph advance the plot? In what way does the Trojans' response in this paragraph build suspense? Highlight evidence from the text and make annotations to note details that support your answer.

5. The last paragraph of the story is a long, detailed battle scene. How do the descriptive details contribute to your understanding of what happens? How does the Trojan War relate to *Black Ships Before Troy*, another selection in this unit? Highlight specific evidence from the text and make annotations to note your ideas.

WRITING PROMPT

The previous excerpt in this unit, *Black Ships Before Troy,* and this excerpt tell the beginning and ending of a long, complicated tale. Many events happened in the middle of the story to bring the plot line from a wedding feast to a bloody battle. Using clues and characters from both excerpts, write a summary of what you think might have happened from the time Paris makes his choice to the beginning of the long war. What caused the war, who were the key players and what was the role of the gods and goddesses in the story plot? Be sure to reference events from both excerpts to tie your story together.

THE HERO SCHLIEMANN:
THE DREAMER WHO DUG FOR TROY

NON-FICTION
Laura Amy Schlitz
2006

INTRODUCTION

Author Laura Amy Schlitz's engaging book tells the story of German businessman and archaeologist Heinrich Schliemann, who was born to explore. As a boy, Schliemann thrilled over Homer's stories in *The Iliad* and *The Odyssey*. As a young man in the import trade, he traveled the globe, learning to speak fourteen languages along the way. By age forty-six, the wealthy

"He was digging into a wall when he caught a glimpse of shining gold."

FIRST READ

From Chapter V

1. When Heinrich began digging at Hissarlik, he had very little idea what he was doing. He knew that he wanted to dig into the mound and find a city of the Bronze Age, but he didn't know what a Bronze Age city would look like. His guide was Homer—he was looking for **artifacts** and **architecture** that matched the descriptions in Homer's poetry. This was not a scientific approach.

2. The thrust of his plan was to dig—deep. At the top of the mound, he expected to find a Roman city, then a Greek city underneath, then a Greek city from the time of Homer, and, just below that, the walled city of *The Iliad*. Instead of carefully sifting through the mound, layer by layer, he decided to dig out vast trenches—rather as if he were removing slices from a cake. Since Homer's Troy was ancient, Heinrich expected to find it near the bottom.

3. And so he dug, violently and impatiently. Frank Calvert advised him to proceed with care, to sift through what he was throwing away, but Heinrich was not a cautious man. He whacked away at the mound as if it were a piñata.

4. Modern **archaeologists** do not dig like this. They remove the earth gently and keep detailed records of what they find. If they find an artifact that isn't what they're hoping to find, they don't discard the artifact: they change their ideas. Instead of looking *for* something, they examine whatever comes to light. Heinrich, of course, was looking for Homer's Troy. "Troy…was sacked twice," modern archaeologists remark, "once by the Greeks and once by Heinrich Schliemann." It is generally agreed that Schliemann did more damage than the Greeks.

…

5   It was not until 1873 that Heinrich found the riches his heart craved. According to Heinrich, the treasure was found on the last morning of May. He was digging into a wall when he caught a glimpse of shining gold. Some instinct told him there was a rich treasure hidden within the wall, and he resolved to dig it out for himself. He announced to his workers that it was his birthday (it wasn't) and told them to take the day off. He summoned Sophia to his side and told her to fetch her red shawl. Together, the husband-and-wife team worked to dig the artifacts out of the wall. There were thousands of precious objects: helmets and swords, **vessels** of gold and silver, shields, lances, vases, cauldrons, and jewelry. There were more than eight thousand gold rings; there were earrings and bracelets and necklaces and diadems.

6   Sophia bundled the treasure in her shawl and carried it back to their living quarters. Once they were alone together, Heinrich decked his beautiful wife in the golden **diadem** that had once kissed the brow of Helen of Troy.

7   This is a good story. It is still found in books, but it is not true. For one thing, Sophia Schliemann was not with her husband on May 31. Her father had recently died, and she had gone to Athens for the funeral. As early as December 1873, Heinrich admitted to a friend at the British Museum that he had made up the story of Sophia and her red shawl. He explained that Sophia was becoming a gifted archaeologist and he wanted to encourage her by including her in the story of his great discovery.

Excerpted from *The Hero Schliemann: The Dreamer Who Dug for Troy* by Laura Amy Schlitz, published by Laurel-Leaf Books.

THINK QUESTIONS

1. What did Heinrich Schliemann hope to find, and why? Use textual evidence to support your answer.

2. How did Schliemann's archaeological methods differ from those of modern archaeologists? Support your answer with textual evidence.

3. Why did Schliemann lie about the circumstances surrounding the discovery of Troy? Cite textual evidence in your response.

4. Remember that the suffix *-ology* means "study or science of," the suffix *-ist* means "one who practices," and the Greek root *arch* means "primitive or original." Use these affix and root meanings, along with the context clues provided in the passage, to determine the meaning of **archaeologists.** Write your definition of "archaeologists" and tell how you got it.

5. Use context to determine the meaning of the word **diadem** as it is used in *The Hero Schliemann: The Dreamer Who Dug for Troy*. Write your definition of "diadem" and tell how you arrived at it.

STUDYSYNC LIBRARY | The Hero Schliemann: The Dreamer Who Dug for Troy

CLOSE READ

Reread the excerpt from *The Hero Schliemann: The Dreamer Who Dug for Troy*. As you reread, complete the Focus Questions below. Then use your answers and annotations from the questions to help you complete the Writing Prompt.

FOCUS QUESTIONS

1. Analyze the point of view the author conveys regarding Schliemann's archaeological methods in paragraph 1. How does she convey this point of view? What role does figurative language play in expressing or supporting that point of view? Highlight textual evidence and make annotations to explain your choices.

2. In paragraphs 3 and 4, the author contrasts the way Schliemann digs with the way that modern archaeologists dig. Highlight evidence from the text that helps you understand the term "archaeological dig," and use that understanding to state whether or not you think Schliemann is conducting one. Make annotations to support your ideas.

3. Highlight the claim the author makes in paragraph 4. How does she use reasons and evidence within the paragraph to support it? Make annotations and highlight textual evidence that supports your ideas.

4. In paragraph 4, the author quotes the viewpoint of modern archaeologists in reference to Heinrich Schliemann. How does the language in this paragraph compare or contrast with the figurative language used to describe Schliemann's methods in earlier paragraphs? Why are the archaeologists using the term *sacked* here? Highlight textual evidence to support your response.

5. Discuss Heinrich Schliemann's life and work in relation to the essential question for this unit: *How does history inform and inspire us?* Make annotations and highlight textual evidence that supports your ideas.

WRITING PROMPT

In *The Hero Schliemann: The Dreamer Who Dug for Troy*, the author acknowledges Schliemann's limitations as an archaeologist. Identify how the author's choice of facts to describe Schliemann's motivations, instincts, and actions reflects Schliemann's unconventional and often problematic methods of discovery. Include in your response an analysis of how the author uses language, including figurative language, to support her claims about Schliemann's work. How do both the author's choice of facts and use of language support her point of view? Support your writing with evidence from the text.

STUDYSYNC LIBRARY | Extended Writing Project

LITERARY ANALYSIS

WRITING PROMPT

Despite all the advances of modern life, we continue to draw inspiration from the ancient world. Ancient culture's influence is visible in our modern-day words and expressions, mythological references, laws, and values. Draw on a theme, idea, or lesson expressed in selections from this unit to write a literary analysis that demonstrates how ancient culture continues to shape the modern world.

Your literary analysis should include:

- an introduction that states a claim, or an opinion, about the themes or central ideas in one or more literary texts
- body paragraphs that feature reasons and relevant evidence from a literary text or texts that support the claim
- a conclusion that follows from the body of the analysis

A literary analysis considers the themes and central ideas of a piece or several pieces of literature. A literary analysis examines connections between different texts, between authors and their texts, and between literature and the world. These connections help readers better understand and identify with what they're reading.

Literary analysis is a form of argumentative writing: The writer makes a claim about the literature and then provides reasons and evidence—details, descriptions, and quotations—to support the claim. After first introducing the claim, the writer develops his or her ideas in the body of the literary analysis, using transitions to link related ideas. The purpose of the literary analysis is for the writer to convince readers that his or her claim about the literature is valid.

STUDYSYNC LIBRARY | **Extended Writing Project**

The features of a literary analysis include:
- an introduction that states a claim, or an opinion, about the text or texts
- a logical organizational structure with clear transitions
- embedded quotations from the text or texts that are clearly cited
- other supporting details or descriptions from the text or texts
- precise language
- a concluding statement

As you continue working on this Extended Writing Project, you'll learn more about crafting each of the elements of a literary analysis.

STUDENT MODEL

Before you get started on your own literary analysis, begin by reading this literary analysis that one student wrote in response to the writing prompt. As you read this Student Model, highlight and annotate the features of a literary analysis that the student included.

The Consequences of Thoughtlessness

People still love reading the myths and tales of ancient Greece. By reading epics about the Trojan War, Perseus's quest, and the simple fables of Aesop, readers today can discover—and perhaps learn from—the Greeks' most deeply cherished values. The Greeks expected their heroes to be not only brave, but also intelligent and patient. To reinforce the point, ancient Greek myths and fables are full of characters who pay dearly for their foolish decisions. One theme of ancient Greek texts is clear: There can be negative consequences if people act without thinking.

Aesop was a sage whose tales were used to teach people lessons about life. Often, the lesson focused on an animal character that acts on impulse. The fox in "The Swollen Fox" was moved by hunger. He crawled into a tree to eat a meal left there by some shepherds. The fox impatiently devoured the food, and as a result became so bloated that he got stuck in the tree's trunk. Another fox told him he would have to remain there "until you become such as you were when you crept in"—in other words, until he was starving (Aesop). Similarly, the flies in "The Flies and the Honey-Pot" were greedy about food. They swarmed a jar of honey to enjoy its sweetness but became stuck and soon died. The lesson was clearly spelled out at the end: "Pleasure bought with pains, hurts" (Aesop). These fables suggest that in seeking pleasure, people may act without thinking, often with unfortunate results.

According to Greek myth, the Trojan War itself was started and concluded by a thoughtless act. When three quarreling goddesses—Hera, Athena, and Aphrodite—tossed a golden apple to a young Trojan named Paris, he caught it without thinking. Each goddess promised him something great if he would choose her as "the fairest" (Sutcliff). As the narrator of *Black Ships Before Troy* explains, instead of acting thoughtfully Paris was impulsive. He "forgot the other two with their offers of wisdom and power" (Sutcliff). He also forgot the nymph he loved and "gave the golden apple to Aphrodite" (Sutcliff). As a result, Paris received what Aphrodite had promised him, and this promise ultimately led to the war between Greece and Troy.

Unlike Paris and the fox, Perseus, as described in *Heroes Every Child Should Know*, knew that it was important to think before acting. Before he began his quest to kill the monster Medusa, Athene told him: "Be patient, and listen; for if you forget my words you will indeed die" (Mabie). Perseus listened carefully about how to use Athene's polished shield to protect himself from Medusa's deadly gaze. He followed Athene's commands even when he was afraid: "Perseus looked down the cliff and shuddered; but he was ashamed to show his dread. Then he thought of Medusa and the renown before him, and he leapt into the empty air" (Mabie). Each time Perseus faced an obstacle, he paused to consider how to go forward, and each time he was successful. Even before he cut off Medusa's head, he "thought awhile with himself, and remembered Athene's words" (Mabie). And by doing so, he successfully became a hero.

One lesson that we can learn from the literature of the ancient Greeks is to think before acting. Many tales that came to us from the Greeks emphasize the terrible consequences of acting thoughtlessly, as Paris did, or impulsively as the hungry fox and the greedy flies did. When individuals act without considering the consequences, they often end up in dire circumstances, sometimes leading to suffering or death, while those who act carefully, with patience and forethought, may become heroes. We might not all become heroes if we stop to reflect before we act, but we will be more likely to avoid trouble. That's an important lesson to think about.

THINK QUESTIONS

1. The writer of the Student Model stated an opinion that a certain theme is clear in many ancient Greek texts. What is the theme, according to the writer, and where in the first paragraph of the Model did the writer state his or her opinion about it?

2. What relevant evidence did the writer include in the Student Model to support his or her opinion? Explain why the evidence is relevant.

3. Write two or three sentences evaluating the writer's conclusion.

4. Thinking about the writing prompt, which selections or other resources would you like to use to write your own literary analysis? What are some of the selections that you may want to analyze in your own literary analysis?

5. Based on the selections you have read, listened to, or researched, how would you answer the question, *What message do ancient texts have for modern readers?* Write two or three sentences stating your opinion about some themes or messages that you might want to consider in the literary analysis you'll be developing.

STUDYSYNC LIBRARY | **Extended Writing Project**

NOTES

PREWRITE

WRITING PROMPT

Despite all the advances of modern life, we continue to draw inspiration from the ancient world. Ancient culture's influence is visible in our modern-day words and expressions, mythological references, laws, and values. Draw on a theme, idea, or lesson expressed in selections from this unit to write a literary analysis that demonstrates how ancient culture continues to shape the modern world.

Your literary analysis should include:

- an introduction that states a claim, or an opinion, about the themes or central ideas in one or more literary texts
- body paragraphs that feature reasons and relevant evidence from a literary text or texts that support the claim
- a conclusion that follows from the body of the analysis

You have been reading about different themes, ideas, and lessons featured in the texts of ancient civilizations. In this Extended Writing Project, you will refer to these themes and teachings as you craft your own literary analysis.

You'll first want to consider the themes, ideas, and lessons featured in the texts from this unit. What happened in each text? What conflict did the text discuss? How did the characters react? What were the consequences of the characters' actions? What lesson does the text teach?

Make a list of the answers to these questions for at least three texts from the unit. As you list the answers, look for patterns between the texts. Are any of the characters' experiences similar? Do the texts teach similar lessons? Identifying patterns can help you decide what you want to discuss in the literary analysis. Use this model to help you get started with your own prewriting:

Text: *Aesop's Fables*

What Happened: A group of flies found an overturned pot of honey and ate it greedily. They became so covered with honey that they could not fly, and as a result died.

Lesson Taught: Acting hastily, without thinking, can bring about destruction.

After you have completed your prewriting, consider your thoughts and ideas as you work through the following Skills lessons to help you map out your analysis.

STUDYSYNC LIBRARY | Extended Writing Project

NOTES

SKILL: THESIS STATEMENT

DEFINE

In informative writing, a thesis statement expresses a writer's main idea about a topic. In argumentative writing, the thesis statement takes the form of a claim. The claim is the writer's opinion about the topic of his or her essay. When composing a literary analysis, a writer expresses an opinion about the themes or central ideas of one or more pieces of literature or informational texts. The claim typically appears in the introduction of the literary analysis, often as its last sentence. Support for the claim, such as text quotations, descriptions, and other details, appears in the body of the literary analysis.

IDENTIFICATION AND APPLICATION

A thesis statement or claim in a literary analysis:

- expresses an opinion about literary or informational texts
- previews what will appear in the body of the literary analysis
- addresses all aspects of the literary analysis prompt
- appears in the introduction paragraph

MODEL

The following is the introduction paragraph from the Student Model, "The Consequences of Thoughtlessness":

> People still love reading the myths and tales of ancient Greece. By reading epics about the Trojan war, Perseus's quest, and the simple fables of Aesop, readers today can discover—and perhaps learn from—the Greeks' most deeply cherished values. The Greeks expected their heroes to be not only brave, but also intelligent and patient. To reinforce the point, ancient Greek

myths and fables are full of characters who pay dearly for their foolish decisions. **One theme of ancient Greek texts is clear: There can be negative consequences if people act without thinking.**

Notice the boldfaced claim. This student's claim responds to the prompt by addressing the topic of themes in ancient texts. It also states the writer's opinion about the topic—that one clear theme of ancient Greek texts is that negative consequences can occur if someone acts without thinking.

 PRACTICE

Write a thesis statement for your literary analysis that articulates your claim in relation to the essay prompt. When you are finished, trade with a partner and offer each other feedback. How clear was the writer's claim? Is it obvious what this literary analysis will focus on? Does it specifically address the prompt? Offer each other suggestions, and remember that they are most helpful when they are constructive.

STUDYSYNC LIBRARY | **Extended Writing Project**

NOTES

SKILL: ORGANIZE ARGUMENTATIVE WRITING

DEFINE

A literary analysis is a form of argumentative writing that tries to persuade readers to accept the writer's interpretation of the theme of a literary text or the central idea of an informative text. To do so, the writer must organize and present the reasons and relevant evidence—the details and quotations from the text or texts—in a logical and convincing way. The writer must select an **organizational structure** that best suits the argument.

The writer of a literary analysis can choose from a number of organizational structures, including **compare and contrast, order of importance, problem and solution, cause-effect, and chronological order.** Experienced writers use an outline or other graphic organizer to decide how to order and convey their ideas most persuasively.

IDENTIFICATION AND APPLICATION

- When selecting an overall organizational structure for a literary analysis, a writer must consider the big idea he or she is arguing—the claim. Then the writer needs to think about the best way to present the supporting evidence. He or she can do this by asking these questions:
    > To support my idea, will I compare and contrast ideas or details in the text?
    > Is there an order of importance to my evidence? Is some evidence stronger than other evidence? Or does all my evidence support my idea equally well?
    > Will I raise a question or identify a problem in my argument? Do I have supporting evidence that suggests a solution or an answer?
    > Does my supporting evidence suggest a cause or an effect?
    > To support my claim, does it make sense to retell the events from the text or texts in chronological order?

- Writers often use specific cue words and phrases to help readers recognize the organizational structure of their writing:
  > Compare and contrast: *like, unlike, and, both, similar to, different from, while, but, in contrast, although, also*
  > Order of importance: *most, most important, least, least important, first, finally, mainly, to begin with*
  > Problem and solution: *problem, solution, why, how*
  > Cause-effect: *because, as a consequence of, as a result, cause, effect, so*
  > Chronological order: *first, next, then, second, finally*

- Writers are not limited to using only one organizational structure throughout a text. Within a specific section or paragraph, they might use one or more different organizational structures. This does not affect the overall organization, however.

MODEL

During the prewriting stage, the writer of the Student Model discovered that several texts in this unit contained evidence to support two related ideas: The ancient Greeks admired heroes who were brave and intelligent, but they looked down on people who were foolish or thoughtless. The writer realized that he or she would need to contrast the evidence about the heroes with the evidence about the foolish characters. So a comparison-contrast organizational structure best suited this writer's argument.

In paragraph 4 of the Student Model, the writer makes the overall comparison-contrast organizational structure explicit through the use of an important cue word:

> **Unlike** Paris and the fox, Perseus, as described in *Heroes Every Child Should Know,* knew that it was important to think before acting. . . .

Once a writer has selected the most appropriate organizational structure, he or she can use an outline or a graphic organizer (for example, a Venn diagram, concept map, or flow chart) to begin organizing the supporting evidence.

The writer of the Student Model used this graphic organizer during planning to organize the evidence that supported this claim: The ancient Greeks believed that acting without thinking resulted in negative consequences.

STUDYSYNC LIBRARY | **Extended Writing Project**

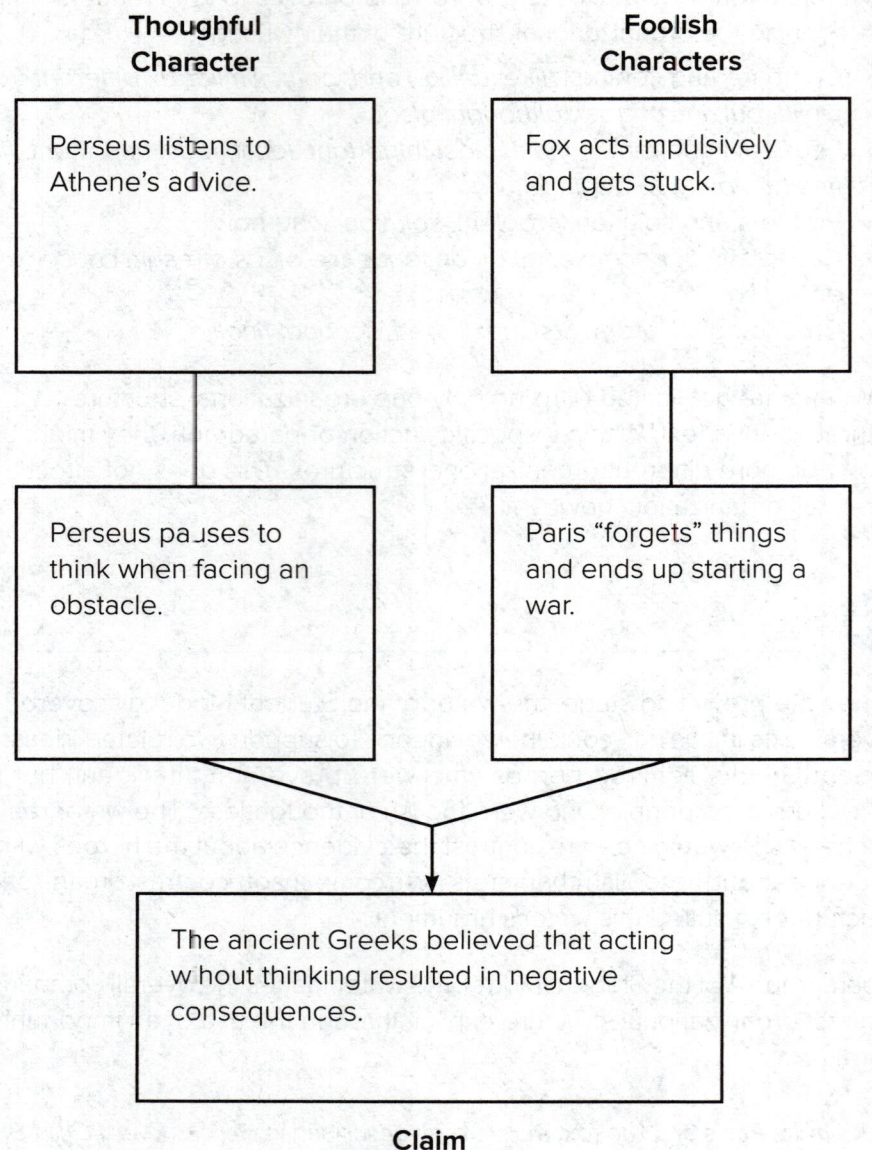

PRACTICE

Using an *Organize Argumentative Writing* graphic organizer like the one used with the Student Model, fill in the information you gathered in the prewrite stage of writing your literary analysis.

STUDYSYNC LIBRARY | Extended Writing Project

SKILL: SUPPORTING DETAILS

★ DEFINE

Because a literary analysis makes a claim about themes in literature or the central ideas in informative texts, it is a form of argumentative writing. To make his or her argument effective, the writer of a literary analysis must provide **supporting details** in the form of **reasons and relevant textual evidence** to add credibility to the claim. Reasons are statements that answer the question "Why?" Writers provide reasons to support a claim and to help readers understand their interpretation of the theme or central idea in a text. Relevant evidence includes definitions, quotations, observations, and examples from the text or texts being analyzed. Relevant evidence is the key to the success of the argument. It makes the reasons more credible and persuasive to the reader, develops the ideas, and clarifies the writer's understanding and interpretation of the text. Without reasons and relevant evidence, the writer would simply be stating his or her opinion about a theme or a central idea.

Because writers want to convince readers that their interpretations of a text's themes or central ideas are credible, they carefully select and present the evidence. Evidence is relevant only if it supports the claim and helps build the argument. If the evidence—a detail, an example, or a quotation—does not support the claim or validate the argument, it is irrelevant and should not be used.

••• IDENTIFICATION AND APPLICATION

Step 1:

Review your claim. To identify supporting details that are relevant to your claim, ask the following question: What am I trying to persuade my audience to believe? A writer might be making a claim about the Egyptian ruler Hatshepsut, for example:

By taking over the throne after her husband's death, Hatshepsut set an important precedent for women.

Step 2:
Ask what a reader needs to know about the topic in order to understand the claim about the theme or central idea. To understand a statement about the precedent Hatshepsut set, for example, a reader must first know what that precedent was. Why was it so significant that Hatshepsut took over the throne? The writer explains the reason for its importance in the following sentence:

Before Hatshepsut's crowning, no woman had ever been pharaoh of Egypt.

The writer then supplies additional details:

In fact, ancient Egypt did not even have a word for a female ruler.

Why is this important? The writer gives more information:

Though the word *pharaoh* meant "king," Hatshepsut nonetheless took the title because she had no other choice.

Step 3:
Look for definitions, quotations, examples, and descriptions to reinforce your claim. Use supporting details like these to build on information you've already provided, but remember to evaluate their relevance to your claim. To do this, ask yourself the following questions:

- Does this information help the reader understand the topic?
- Does this information support my claim?
- Does this information help build my argument?
- Is there stronger evidence that makes the same point?

MODEL

In the following excerpt from *A Short Walk Around the Pyramids & Through the World of Art* Philip M. Isaacson develops the claim that the ancient Egyptian pyramids at Giza "create three unforgettable works of art."

What do we learn about art when we look at the pyramids?

First, when all of the things that go into a work—its components—complement one another, they create an object that has a certain spirit, and we can call that spirit *harmony*. The pyramids are harmonious because **limestone, a warm, quiet material, is a cordial companion for a simple, logical, pleasing shape. In fact, the stone and the shape** are so comfortable with each other that the pyramids seem inevitable—as though they were bound to have the form, color, and texture that they do have.

The pyramids also show us that simple things must be made with care. The fine workmanship that went into the building of the pyramids is a part of their beauty. Complicated shapes may conceal poor work—such shapes distract our eye—**but in something as simple as a pyramid, there is no way to hide flaws. Because any flaw would mar its beauty, the craftsmanship must be perfect** . . . Any building less beautifully designed or made with less skill would have looked awkward in the company of the dignified old structures near it.

Finally, pyramids show us that light helps to shape our feelings about art. **As the sun moves above the desert, the pyramids seem to change.** As they do, our feelings about them also change. In the **early morning** they sit squarely on the horizon, and we feel that they have **become the kings** for which they were named; by midday they have become restless and change into **silver-white clouds**; and at **dusk** they settle down and **regain their power**.

In paragraph 2, Isaacson addresses his first reason why he believes the pyramids are works of art: they're harmonious. He then gives relevant evidence that supports why.

In paragraph 3, Isaacson addresses his second reason why the pyramids are works of art: their fine workmanship. He provides relevant evidence that supports his ideas about this.

In paragraph 4, Isaacson addresses his third reason why he thinks the pyramids are works of art: they change with the light. He then gives relevant evidence that supports the different ways they do this.

The supporting details Isaacson provides add credibility to his claim.

PRACTICE

Review a text you plan to include in your literary analysis. Then choose a detail from the text that supports the claim you plan to make. Write three or four sentences telling why this specific detail is relevant and important evidence that will support your reasons and claim in your literary analysis.

STUDYSYNC LIBRARY | **Extended Writing Project**

NOTES

PLAN

WRITING PROMPT

Despite all the advances of modern life, we continue to draw inspiration from the ancient world. Ancient culture's influence is visible in our modern-day words and expressions, mythological references, laws, and values. Draw on a theme, idea, or lesson expressed in selections from this unit to write a literary analysis that demonstrates how ancient culture continues to shape the modern world.

Your literary analysis should include:

- an introduction that states a claim, or an opinion, about the themes or central ideas in one or more literary texts
- body paragraphs that feature reasons and relevant evidence from a literary text or texts that support the claim
- a conclusion that follows from the body of the analysis

Review the information you listed in your *Organize Argumentative Writing* graphic organizer detailing events and characters from different texts, along with a theme or lesson the texts share. This organized information and the claim you made in your thesis statement will help you to create a road map to use for writing your literary analysis.

Consider the following questions as you develop your main paragraph topics and their supporting details in the road map:

- What happened in the texts?
- What conflicts did the texts discuss?
- How did the characters react?
- What were the consequences of the characters' actions?
- What lesson did the texts teach, or what was their theme?
- How do the texts' lessons still shape the modern world?

When you plan your literary analysis, you want to be sure that the main topic of each paragraph supports or gives a reason for your claim. You also want to be sure that the ideas and details you include in each paragraph, such as the textual evidence you cite from your sources, are relevant to that paragraph's specific topic and help your readers understand the topic. Use this model to get started with your road map:

Literary Analysis Road Map

Claim: One theme of ancient Greek texts is that negative consequences can occur if people act without thinking.

Paragraph 1 Topic: People can discover and learn about ancient Greeks' values by reading their tales.

>**Supporting Detail #1:** Greeks expected heroes to be brave, intelligent, and patient.

>**Supporting Detail #2:** Characters who were foolish paid dearly for it.

Paragraph 2 Topic: Aesop's tales taught lessons about what happened to greedy characters.

>**Supporting Detail #1:** The fox in "The Swollen Fox" ate too much after finding food hidden in a tree. He got stuck in the tree.

>**Supporting Detail #2:** The flies in "The Flies and the Honey-Pot" swarmed a jar of honey and got stuck. They soon died.

Paragraph 3 Topic: A thoughtless act started the Trojan War.

>**Supporting Detail #1:** The goddesses Hera, Athena, and Aphrodite asked the Trojan, Paris, to choose which of them was the fairest. Paris chose Aphrodite.

>**Supporting Detail #2:** As a result, Paris received what Aphrodite had promised him, and this promise ultimately led to the war between Greece and Troy.

STUDYSYNC LIBRARY | **Extended Writing Project**

SKILL: INTRODUCTIONS

⭐ DEFINE

The **introduction** is the opening paragraph or section of a literary analysis or other nonfiction text. The introduction of a literary analysis **identifies the texts or the topic to be discussed, states the writer's claim,** and **previews the supporting evidence** that will appear in the body of the text. The introduction is also the place where most writers include a **"hook"** that is intended to connect with and engage readers.

••• IDENTIFICATION AND APPLICATION

- In a literary analysis, the introduction is the section in which the writer **identifies the texts or topic to be discussed.** Remember, a literary analysis examines one or more literary texts, and the writer must let readers know what the focus of the analysis will be. Once readers have that information, they can concentrate on the writer's claim.

- A literary analysis is a form of argument, so the writer's claim is an important part of the introduction. The claim is a direct statement of the writer's opinion about or interpretation of the texts under discussion. By **stating the claim** in the introduction, the writer lets readers know the ideas he or she will explore in the body of the analysis. Establishing a claim here also allows readers to form their own opinions, which they can then measure against the writer's as they read the literary analysis.

- Another use of the introduction is to provide a **preview of the supporting evidence** that will follow in the body of the text. By using the introduction to hint at key details, the writer can establish an effective argument, increasing the likelihood that readers will agree with his or her claim.

- The introduction's **"hook"** leaves readers with a first impression about what to expect from the writer. Good hooks engage readers' interest and make them want to keep reading. A hook might be an intriguing image, a surprising detail, a funny anecdote, or a shocking statistic. The hook should appeal to the audience and help readers connect to the topic in a meaningful way so that they will take the writer's claim seriously.

MODEL

The introduction of the excerpt from *A Short Walk Around the Pyramids & Through the World of Art* by Philip M. Isaacson contains key elements of an introduction:

> **At Giza, a few miles north of Saqqara, sit three great pyramids,** each named for the king—or Pharaoh—during whose reign it was built. No other buildings are so well known, yet the first sight of them sitting in their field is breathtaking. When you walk among them, you walk in a place made for giants. **They seem too large to have been made by human beings, too perfect to have been formed by nature, and when the sun is overhead, not solid enough to be attached to the sand.** In the minutes before sunrise, they are the color of faded roses, and when the last rays of the desert sun touch them, they turn to amber. But whatever the light, **their broad proportions, the beauty of the limestone, and the care with which it is fitted into place create three unforgettable works of art.**

In this introductory paragraph, the writer immediately identifies his **topic**—the pyramids of Giza. He provides a **hook** by describing the pyramids in vivid detail: they seem "too large," "too perfect," and "not solid enough to be attached to the sand." These details lead directly to the writer's **claim**—that the pyramids are "unforgettable works of art." The writer also hints at the **evidence** to follow in the analysis, referring to the pyramids' "broad proportions," "the beauty of the limestone," and "the care with which it is fitted into place."

 PRACTICE

Write an introduction for your literary analysis that includes the claim you have already worked on and a hook to capture your readers' interest. When you are finished, trade with a peer review partner. Provide helpful feedback on each other's introductions.

STUDYSYNC LIBRARY | **Extended Writing Project**

SKILL: BODY PARAGRAPHS AND TRANSITIONS

 DEFINE

Body paragraphs are the parts of a literary analysis that appear between the introduction and conclusion paragraphs. This is the section where you support your claim with reasons and evidence taken from the text or texts you are writing about. In general, each body paragraph should focus on one main point or idea so that the reader can easily follow along. All the main points of the body paragraphs should collectively support the claim.

It's important to structure each body paragraph clearly. One possible way to structure the body paragraph of a literary analysis is by including the following elements:

> **Topic sentence:** The topic sentence is the first sentence of a body paragraph. It states the main point of the paragraph. The topic sentence should relate to the claim you make in your introduction.
>
> **Evidence #1:** You should provide carefully selected evidence from the text or texts to support your topic sentence. Evidence can include relevant definitions, specific details, quotations, and examples.
>
> **Evidence #2:** Continue to develop your topic sentence with a second piece of evidence.
>
> **Analysis/Explanation:** After presenting evidence, you should explain how the evidence helps support your topic sentence—and general claim—about the text or texts.
>
> **Concluding sentence:** After presenting your evidence and analysis, wrap up the main idea in a concluding sentence.

Transitions are connecting words and phrases that writers use to clarify the relationship among ideas in a text. For example, transition words and phrases can help clarify the relationship among a claim, reasons, and evidence in a literary analysis. Transitions help make connections between words in a sentence and ideas in individual paragraphs.

Words such as *and, or,* and *but* help writers make connections between words in a sentence, while words and phrases such as *also, in addition to,* and *likewise* help establish relationships between ideas in body paragraphs. Adding transition words or phrases like these to the beginning or end of a paragraph can help a writer guide readers smoothly through a text.

Writers also use words and phrases such as *unlike, similarly, in contrast, most important,* and *least important* to help indicate the organizational structure in which they're presenting ideas. *Unlike, similarly,* and *in contrast,* for example, indicate a compare-and-contrast relationship among ideas. In a literary analysis, writers often compare and contrast texts in terms of the texts' similar or different approaches to a common theme, character, or other element.

 ## IDENTIFICATION AND APPLICATION

- Body paragraphs are the section of the literary analysis between the introduction and conclusion paragraphs. These paragraphs provide the main points of the literary analysis, along with their evidence and explanations. Typically, writers develop one main idea per body paragraph.
  › A topic sentence clearly states the main idea of that paragraph. The main idea always relates to the writer's claim.
  › Evidence consists of relevant definitions, specific details, quotations, and examples.
  › Analysis and explanation tell how the evidence relates to the topic sentence.
  › A conclusion sentence wraps up the paragraph's main idea.
- Certain transition words and phrases indicate specific organizational relationships within a text. Here are some examples:
  › Cause-effect: *because, accordingly, as a result, so, for, since, therefore, if, then*
  › Compare and contrast: *like, unlike, also, both, similarly, although, while, but, however, whereas, meanwhile, on the contrary, yet, still*
  › Chronological order: *first, then, next, finally, before, after, when, following, and within a few years*

 ## MODEL

Each body paragraph of the Student Model develops and supports the writer's claim with textual evidence. Just as a reader draws evidence from a literary or informational text to support ideas in a discussion, a writer also selects specific textual evidence to support ideas in his or her writing.

NOTES

Read the first body paragraph from the Student Model, "The Consequences of Thoughtlessness." Look closely at the structure and note the textual evidence as well as the transition word in bold. Think about the effectiveness of the literary analysis. Does it develop the main point made in the topic sentence? How does the transition word help you understand the relationship between the writer's claim and the ideas developed in the body paragraph?

> **Aesop was a sage whose tales were used to teach people lessons about life.** Often, the lesson focused on an animal character that acts on impulse. The fox in "The Swollen Fox" was moved by hunger. He crawled into a tree to eat a meal left there by some shepherds. The fox impatiently devoured the food, and as a result became so bloated that he got stuck in the tree's trunk. Another fox told him he would have to remain there **"until you become such as you were when you crept in"**—in other words, until he was starving (Aesop). **Similarly,** the flies in "The Flies and the Honey-Pot" were greedy about food. They swarmed a jar of honey to enjoy its sweetness but became stuck and soon died. The lesson was clearly spelled out at the end: **"Pleasure bought with pains, hurts"** (Aesop). These fables suggest that in seeking pleasure, people may act without thinking, often with unfortunate results.

The first body paragraph of the Student Model begins by stating, "Aesop was a sage whose tales were used to teach people lessons about life." This **topic sentence** clearly establishes the main idea this body paragraph will develop. It lets readers know that the writer will be discussing the lessons Aesop's tales taught.

This topic sentence is followed by **evidence.** The writer cites the example of what happens to the greedy fox in "The Swollen Fox" by including a direct quotation from the tale. The writer then cites the example of the flies in the fable "The Flies and the Honey-Pot." By using the transition word *similarly,* the writer lets readers know that the the flies are being compared to the fox. The writer chooses a direct quotation from this second fable to highlight the similarity in the lesson learned by the fox and the flies: "Pleasure bought with pains, hurts" (Aesop).

Next, the writer **explains** the significance of these ancient tales and what they tell us. The paragraph concludes by stating that Aesop's fables suggest that "in seeking gratification, people may act without thinking, often with unfortunate results." This **concluding sentence** wraps up the paragraph and relates back to the claim that a common theme in ancient Greek texts was that thoughtlessness led to bad consequences.

The writer uses additional transition words and phrases such as *also, but,* and *then* within the other body paragraphs to help guide readers as they transition from one sentence to the next.

 PRACTICE

Write one body paragraph for your literary analysis that compares or contrasts the texts selected for your essay. Make sure your paragraph follows the suggested format, starting with a topic sentence. When you are finished, trade with a partner and offer each other feedback. How effective is the topic sentence at stating the main point of the paragraph? How strong is the textual evidence used to support the topic sentence? What is being compared and contrasted in the paragraph? Do transition words help make the compare-and-contrast relationship clear? Offer each other suggestions, and remember that they are most helpful when they are constructive.

STUDYSYNC LIBRARY | Extended Writing Project

SKILL: CONCLUSIONS

DEFINE

A **conclusion** is the closing statement or section of a nonfiction text. In a literary analysis, the conclusion brings the writer's argument to a close. It follows directly from the introduction's claim and the reasons and relevant evidence provided in the body of the text. The conclusion of a literary analysis should restate the claim the writer is making about the text or texts in the analysis and also summarize the writer's main ideas. In some types of writing, the conclusion might also include a recommendation, a call to action, or an insightful comment.

IDENTIFICATION AND APPLICATION

- An effective conclusion of a literary analysis will restate the writer's claim about the themes or central ideas of one or more texts.
- The conclusion should briefly summarize the strongest and most convincing reasons and evidence from the body paragraphs. Focusing on the strongest points makes it more likely that readers will agree with the writer's claim.
- Some conclusions offer a recommendation or some form of insight relating to the analysis. This may take any of the following forms:
  > An answer to a question first posed in the introduction
  > A question designed to elicit reflection on the part of the reader
  > A memorable or inspiring message
  > A last compelling example
  > A suggestion that readers learn more

MODEL

In the concluding paragraph of the student model "The Consequences of Thoughtlessness," the writer reinforces the claim, reminds readers of the main points of the literary analysis, and ends with a strong final message.

> **One lesson that we can learn from the literature of the ancient Greeks is to think before acting.** Many tales that came to us from the Greeks emphasize the **terrible consequences of acting thoughtlessly, as Paris did, or impulsively as the hungry fox and the greedy flies did. When individuals act without considering the consequences, they often end up in dire circumstances, sometimes leading to suffering or death,** while those who act carefully, with patience and forethought, may become heroes. We might not all become heroes **if we stop to reflect before we do something, but we will be more likely to avoid trouble. That's an important lesson to think about.**

The claim in the student model's introduction states that one theme of ancient Greek texts is that negative consequences can result if you act without thinking. The first line of the conclusion above mentions that we can learn from ancient Greek literature to think before acting. In the next few sentences, the writer includes specific examples of characters who suffered as a result of their thoughtlessness. Next, the writer states, "When individuals act without considering the consequences, they often end up suffering or dead." This statement directly supports the claim of the literary analysis. At the very end, the writer leaves us with a final message to apply to our own lives, stating that, "if we stop to reflect before we do something . . . we will be more likely to avoid trouble." This is an effective message to leave with readers.

PRACTICE

Write a conclusion for your literary analysis. Your literary analysis should include a restatement of the claim you have already worked on and a final thought you want to leave with readers. When you are finished, trade with a peer review partner. Offer each other supportive feedback on your conclusions.

STUDYSYNC LIBRARY | Extended Writing Project

NOTES

DRAFT

WRITING PROMPT

Despite all the advances of modern life, we continue to draw inspiration from the ancient world. Ancient culture's influence is visible in our modern-day words and expressions, mythological references, laws, and values. Draw on a theme, idea, or lesson expressed in selections from this unit to write a literary analysis that demonstrates how ancient culture continues to shape the modern world.

Your literary analysis should include:

- an introduction that states a claim, or an opinion, about the themes or central ideas in one or more literary texts
- body paragraphs that feature reasons and relevant evidence from a literary text or texts that support the claim
- a conclusion that follows from the body of the analysis

You've already begun working on your own literary analysis. You've considered your purpose, audience, and topic. You've carefully examined the unit's texts and selected the ones you plan to write about. Based on your analysis of textual evidence, you've identified what you want to say about lessons expressed in the texts. You've decided how to organize information, and you've gathered supporting details in the form of reasons and relevant evidence. You've practiced writing drafts of an introduction, a body paragraph, and a conclusion. Now it's time to write a whole draft of your literary analysis.

Use your road map and your other prewriting materials to help you as you write. Remember that a literary analysis begins with an introduction that features a claim. Body paragraphs then develop the claim by providing reasons and relevant evidence to support it, such as quotations, specific details, and examples. Transitional words and phrases establish an organizational structure and help the reader understand the relationships among the claim, reasons, and evidence in the literary analysis. A concluding paragraph restates or reinforces the claim and important points from the literary analysis. The conclusion may also convey a message to your readers.

When drafting, ask yourself these questions:

- How can I make my hook more effective?
- What can I do to clarify my claim?
- Which textual evidence—including relevant direct quotations, examples, and observations—best supports my claim?
- How can I improve the analysis by using better transitions?
- How can I effectively restate my claim in the conclusion?
- What final message do I want to leave with my readers?

Be sure to carefully read your draft before you submit it. You want to make sure you've addressed every part of the prompt.

REVISE

WRITING PROMPT

Despite all the advances of modern life, we continue to draw inspiration from the ancient world. Ancient culture's influence is visible in our modern-day words and expressions, mythological references, laws, and values. Draw on a theme, idea, or lesson expressed in selections from this unit to write a literary analysis that demonstrates how ancient culture continues to shape the modern world.

Your literary analysis should include:

- an introduction that states a claim, or an opinion, about the themes or central ideas in one or more literary texts
- body paragraphs that feature reasons and relevant evidence from a literary text or texts that support the claim
- a conclusion that follows from the body of the analysis

You have written a draft of your literary analysis. You have also received input from your peers about how to improve it. Now you are going to revise your draft.

Here are some recommendations to help you revise:

- Review the suggestions made by your peers.
- Focus on maintaining a formal style. A formal style suits your purpose—persuading readers to agree with your ideas about a text or texts. It is also appropriate for your audience—students, teachers, and other readers interested in learning more about your topic. Your style and tone should be consistent throughout your literary analysis.
    > As you revise, eliminate any informal language, such as slang.
    > Remove any first-person pronouns such as "I," "me," or "mine" or instances of addressing readers as "you," except when leaving readers

with a final thought or message in the conclusion. Check that you have used and punctuated all pronouns correctly.
> If necessary, incorporate a greater variety of sentence structures, and check that you aren't beginning every sentence the same way. Varying sentence lengths and patterns will make your writing style more interesting to read.

- After you have revised elements of style, review your literary analysis to see whether you can make improvements to its information or organization.
    > Does your introduction present a claim that is reinforced by your conclusion?
    > Have you chosen clear reasons and relevant evidence to demonstrate how ancient cultures continue to shape the modern world? What new textual evidence might you want to add, such as quotations and examples, to better support your claim?
    > Can you substitute a more precise word for a word that is too general or overused?
    > Is your organizational structure apparent? What transitional words and phrases might help clarify the connection among your claim, reasons, and evidence?

STUDYSYNC LIBRARY | **Extended Writing Project**

SKILL: SOURCES AND CITATIONS

DEFINE

Sources are the texts that writers use to research their writing. A **primary source** is a first-hand account of events by the person who experienced them. Another type of source is known as a **secondary source.** This is a source that analyzes or interprets primary sources. **Citations** are notes that provide information about the source texts. It is necessary for a writer to provide a citation if he or she quotes directly from a text or refers to others' ideas in a text. The citation lets readers know who stated the quoted words or originally came up with the idea.

IDENTIFICATION AND APPLICATION

- Sources can be either primary or secondary. Primary sources are first-hand accounts or original materials, such as the following:
  > Letters or other correspondence
  > Photographs
  > Official documents
  > Diaries or journals
  > Autobiographies or memoirs
  > Eyewitness accounts and interviews
  > Audio recordings and radio broadcasts
  > Literary texts, such as novels, poems, fables, and dramas
  > Works of art
  > Artifacts

- Secondary sources are usually texts. Secondary sources are the written interpretation and analysis of primary source materials. Some examples of secondary sources include:
  > Encyclopedia articles
  > Textbooks
  > Commentary or criticisms

- › Histories
- › Documentary films
- › News analyses

- Whether sources are primary or secondary, they must be **credible** and **accurate.** This means the information in the sources should be reliable.
- When a writer of a literary analysis quotes directly from a source, he or she must copy the words exactly as they appear in the source, placing them within quotation marks. Here's an example from the Student Model:

  He "forgot the other two with their offers of wisdom and power" (Sutcliff). He also forgot the nymph he loved and "gave the golden apple to Aphrodite" (Sutcliff).

- Writers of literary analyses must cite the sources they're quoting directly. One way to do this is by putting the author's name in parentheses at the end of the sentence in which the quotation appears. This is the method shown above in the excerpt from the Student Model. Another method is to cite the author's name in the context of the sentence.
- Writers must also provide citations when borrowing ideas from another source, even when writers are just paraphrasing, or putting the ideas into their own words. Citations serve both to credit the source and help readers find out where they can learn more.

MODEL

In this excerpt from the Student Model, "The Consequences of Thoughtlessness," the writer quotes from the literary text he or she is analyzing and identifies the quotations' source.

> Aesop was a sage whose tales were used to teach people lessons about life. Often, the lesson focused on an animal character that acts on impulse. The fox in "The Swollen Fox" was moved by hunger. He crawled into a tree to eat a meal left there by some shepherds. The fox impatiently devoured the food, and as a result became so bloated that he got stuck in the tree's trunk. Another fox told him he would have to remain there "until you become such as you were when you crept in"—in other words, starving (Aesop). Similarly, the flies in "The Flies and the Honey-Pot" were greedy about food. They

swarmed a jar of honey to enjoy its sweetness but became stuck and soon died. The lesson was clearly spelled out at the end: **"Pleasure bought with pain, hurts" (Aesop).** These fables suggest that in seeking gratification, people may act without thinking, often with unfortunate results.

Notice that only the portions of text taken directly from the source appear in quotations, and that the author's last name appears in parentheses at the end of the sentence in which the quotation appears.

 PRACTICE

Choose a body paragraph from the revised draft of your literary analysis. Be sure it is a paragraph that includes textual evidence in the form of a quotation. Review your body paragraph and add or correct citations of quoted material. Remember that you can cite the author of a source either in the context of the sentence that contains the quoted material or in parentheses at the end of the sentence.

EDIT, PROOFREAD, AND PUBLISH

WRITING PROMPT

Despite all the advances of modern life, we continue to draw inspiration from the ancient world. Ancient culture's influence is visible in our modern-day words and expressions, mythological references, laws, and values. Draw on a theme, idea, or lesson expressed in selections from this unit to write a literary analysis that demonstrates how ancient culture continues to shape the modern world.

Your literary analysis should include:

- an introduction that states a claim, or an opinion, about the themes or central ideas in one or more literary texts
- body paragraphs that feature reasons and relevant evidence from a literary text or texts that support the claim
- a conclusion that follows from the body of the analysis

Now that you have revised your literary analysis and received input from your peers, it's time to edit and proofread to produce a final version. Have you taken into consideration all the suggestions from your peers? Ask yourself these questions: Have I fully supported my claim with strong textual evidence? Have I correctly cited my sources? Does my literary analysis need additional transitions to clarify the relationship among my claim, reasons, and evidence? Have I consistently maintained a formal style? Does my conclusion follow from my analysis of the texts and reinforce my claim? What else can I do to improve my literary analysis?

Once you are satisfied with your work, proofread it for errors. For example, check that you have used correct punctuation for quotations and citations. Have you used pronouns correctly? Have you capitalized all proper nouns? Be sure to correct any misspelled words you find in your literary analysis.

After you have made all your corrections, you are ready to submit and publish your work. You can distribute your writing to family and friends, hang it on a bulletin board, or post your writing on a blog. If you do decide to publish your work online, include links to your sources and citations. This will enable readers to learn more from the sources on their own time. You might also want to adapt your writing to an oral report that you can deliver as a presentation to your class or to an audience of friends or family. As a writer, you want to share your words and thoughts with others.

PHOTO/IMAGE CREDITS:

Cover, ©iStock.com/TerryJLawrence, ©iStock.com/Pakhnyushchyy, ©iStock.com/alexey_boldin, ©iStock.com/skegbydave
p. iii, ©iStock.com/DNY59, ©iStock.com/alexey_boldin, ©iStock.com/LaraBelova
p. iv, E+/Getty Images
p. v, ©iStock.com/moevin, ©iStock.com/skegbydave, ©iStock.com/Chemlamp
p. 2, ©iStock.com/Pakhnyushchyy
p. 4, ©iStock.com/takepicsforfun
p. 10, Print Collector/Getty Images
p. 15, ©iStock.com/cinoby
p. 21, ©iStock.com/karimhesham
p. 26, ©iStock.com/aldra
p. 31, ©iStock.com/ABDESIGN
p. 37, ©iStock.com/timurka
p. 40, ©iStock.com/timurka
p. 48, ©iStock.com/Matt_Gibson
p. 53, ©iStock.com/muratseyit
p. 59, ©iStock.com/klaidas
p. 63, ©iStock.com/moevin, ©iStock.com/svariophoto
p. 64, ©iStock.com/moevin, ©iStock.com/skegbydave
p. 68, ©iStock.com/moevin, ©iStock.com/skegbydave
p. 70, ©iStock.com/Chemlamp, ©iStock.com/skegbydave
p. 72, ©iStock.com/THEPALMER, ©iStock.com/skegbydave
p. 75, ©iStock.com/shaunl, ©iStock.com/skegbydave
p. 78, ©iStock.com/moevin, ©iStock.com/skegbydave
p. 80, ©iStock.com/bo1982, ©iStock.com/skegbydave
p. 82, ©iStock.com/Jeff_Hu, ©iStock.com/skegbydave
p. 86, ©iStock.com/stevedangers, ©iStock.com/skegbydave
p. 88, ©iStock.com/moevin, ©iStock.com/skegbydave
p. 90, ©iStock.com/moevin, ©iStock.com/skegbydave
p. 92, ©iStock.com/mmac72, ©iStock.com/skegbydave
p. 95, ©iStock.com/moevin, ©iStock.com/skegbydave

Text Fulfillment Through StudySync

If you are interested in specific titles, please fill out the form below and we will check availability through our partners.

ORDER DETAILS

Date:

TITLE	AUTHOR	Paperback/ Hardcover	Specific Edition *If Applicable*	Quantity

SHIPPING INFORMATION

Contact:
Title:
School/District:
Address Line 1:
Address Line 2:
Zip or Postal Code:
Phone:
Mobile:
Email:

BILLING INFORMATION ☐ SAME AS SHIPPING

Contact:
Title:
School/District:
Address Line 1:
Address Line 2:
Zip or Postal Code:
Phone:
Mobile:
Email:

PAYMENT INFORMATION

☐ CREDIT CARD

Name on Card:
Card Number: Expiration Date: Security Code:

☐ PO

Purchase Order Number:

StudySync Text Fulfillment, BookheadEd Learning, LLC
610 Daniel Young Drive | Sonoma, CA 95476